# Prospecting
# Hacks

**Foreword By Steve Gordon**

Best Selling Author of *"Unstoppable Referrals"*

# Prospecting

# Hacks

www.ProspectingHacks.com

**The Proven, Fastest Ways To Find New Sales Opportunities Without Buying Ads or Cold Calling.**

Includes AI Hacks For Generating More Leads, Sales and Revenue!

# John Phillippe

Revica.io, LLC
2929 Westheimer, Suite 215
Houston, Texas 77098
United States

www.ProspectingHacks.com

# CONTENTS

Foreword by Steve Gordon ............................................................. 9
Introduction ................................................................................ 11
Why It's Important To Develop Your Prospecting Skills ............... 17
The Prospecting Challenge .......................................................... 20
Make Yourself The "Go-To" Expert ............................................. 25
Identify And Understand Your Prospect Avatar .......................... 29
Create A "Godfather" Offer ......................................................... 34
Perfect Your Elevator Pitch ......................................................... 39
How to Handle Objections During Your Prospecting .................. 46
How to Get Past "Gate Keepers" ................................................. 49
Let's Get Prospect Hacking ......................................................... 54

## ONLINE PROSPECTING

Create An Email List of Potential Clients/Customers ................... 59
Cold Email Prospecting ............................................................... 66
Video Email Prospecting ............................................................. 74
Create An Industry Newsletter .................................................... 86
Be a Guest Writer on an Industry Blog ....................................... 92
Google Alerts .............................................................................. 97
Google Business Profile ............................................................. 103
Social Media ............................................................................. 109
Collaborate with Social Media And Business Influencers ......... 115
Instagram Prospecting .............................................................. 120
Facebook Prospecting ............................................................... 130
LinkedIn Prospecting ................................................................ 135
Tiktok Prospecting .................................................................... 140
Start a YouTube Channel .......................................................... 144
Create a Podcast ....................................................................... 150
Be A Guest on A Podcast .......................................................... 156
AI Chat Bots ............................................................................. 161

# IN-PERSON PROSPECTING

Referrals ........................................................................................ 169
Host an Industry Event ................................................................ 175
Be A Guest Speaker at an Industry Event .............................. 178
Mind Your Surroundings ............................................................ 181

# ALTERNATIVE PROSPECTING

Affiliate Marketing ....................................................................... 187
Snail Mail ....................................................................................... 190
Automated Postcards ................................................................. 198
Write A Book ................................................................................. 201
QR Codes ....................................................................................... 213
Automated Sales Leads 24X7 Using AI ................................... 217
Go Make Money! .......................................................................... 223

Dedicated to Elizabeth and Lindsey, the two hardest-working, most creative sales prospectors I have ever known.

# FOREWORD BY STEVE GORDON

When John told me he wanted to write "yet another book" on prospecting, I thought to myself, what could he possibly bring that's new to a topic that has been written about thousands of times? In fact, as I write this, Amazon lists over 2,000 books on sales prospecting.

So why should you read this one?

Very simply, John has done something unique. The book you're holding in your hands is not going to teach you some all-encompassing prospecting system–in my experience, those rarely work. Instead, John is giving you what every business owner needs...

**An answer to the question, "How can I get a client right now?!"**

You see, those prospecting systems are all great, but no one ever follows them for long. The status quo takes over, or you have a deal fall through, or an unexpected bill comes due, or you just want to make some more money...

Then most business owners (and I've consulted with and coached hundreds) get stumped with what to do to get that next client *fast*.

No more!

Just pick up this book, flip to a page that inspires you, and John will give you a technique you can use TODAY to get in front of a prospect and move the needle.

Now, where should you start? I'd suggest skipping ahead to Page 22 and reading the story of how John turned a "no" sales call into a big "YESSSS!!!" (And it's not what you might think).

Read that first. If that gets you excited for John and his whole approach to prospecting, then go back and read this book cover to cover.

You won't be disappointed.

**Steve Gordon**
5x Bestselling Author
Creator of The Unstoppable Referrals™ Method, and
The Million Dollar Author™ Method


February 1, 2023
Tallahassee, Florida

# INTRODUCTION

*Use this book as an inspirational reference* for when you are stuck on how to get new customers. We have all been there, and it's not a good feeling. This book will hopefully break you out of any prospecting rut you might find yourself in and get you back on the path to making money!

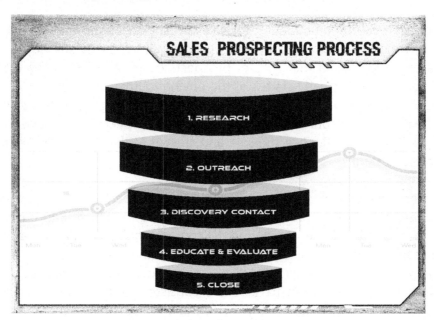

Prospecting is a necessary evil in the sales process, and I can attest to that as someone who has spent the last 38 years (as of this writing) figuring out how to get new clients on my own in various media formats. As a creative and media producer, I would much rather spend my time being efficient and profitable while being as creative as possible, but unfortunately, as a one-man band, I had to get creative with finding new opportunities.

The truth is, without a steady stream of quality leads, no new sales can happen. And while it's traditionally the marketing department's job to generate leads for sales, that doesn't mean sales prospectors should sit around waiting for leads to come to them. They still need to put in the effort to self-generate leads.

But the landscape of prospecting has changed. These days, buyers are more independent and do their own research before contacting a salesperson. A study by CSO Insights found that 45% of prospects preferred to evaluate their needs and search for solutions on their own before reaching out to a salesperson. And that trend has continued. B2B buyers now spend only 17% of their time meeting with sellers and just 5-6% talking to a sales rep when comparing offers. Instead, they turn to the internet and social media to make purchasing decisions.

This shift can be intimidating for sales prospectors, who may feel like they're losing control of the sales process. But there is still hope! A recent study found that 91% of prospects don't mind engaging with a sales rep in the early stages of the buying journey, including 34% of new buyers who are particularly interested in engaging with a sales prospector early on. This means that sales prospectors still have the opportunity to influence the sale and steer it in the right direction in the early stages.

So, how can sales prospectors take hold of the wheel? First, be there for buyers when they need you. Research shows that 60% of B2B buyers want to contact a sales rep during the consideration stage (after they've researched and shortlisted their options). Another strategy is to simply initiate the first contact. Just like you schedule consistent time for workouts, it's important to schedule consistent time for prospecting every day. In fact, 81.6% of top-performing salespeople spend at least 4 hours a day on sales-related activities.

This book is a collection of prospecting techniques I have personally used over the past 38 years. At some point in my career, all *of these techniques made me money*. One of my favorite mentors, Jeffrey Gitomer, once said: "People hate to be sold to, but they love to buy!" So don't get discouraged if you are on a bad streak. Businesses and people both have to buy services and products; that's just the way the world works. Believe me when I tell you there are countless new customers on the planet that can't wait to buy what you are selling. You just have to reach them on their terms, on their platform, and on their time schedule... but they are there.

And my last bit of advice that has always worked for me is to remember this one phrase: "Sell a solution, not a product or service." Potential customers don't care about how long it took you to invent something or how many awards you may have won, they care about how you can solve their problems, and that's what you should focus on when prospecting.

**Good luck using this guide! Go make money!**

 **FROM THE FIELD**

Early in my career, I produced a lot of television, especially commercials. Digital editing was just coming onto the scene, but the bulk of production houses were still trying to maximize the R.O.I. out of their outdated tape machines and edit suites. This was the early '90's. I was fortunate enough to work with a production house that had just acquired one of the very first digitally based edit systems called an "AVID." They let me teach myself how to use it whenever I had the time. It ran on an Apple II with a 12' screen. By default, I found myself to be one of the first commercial digital editors in Texas. Today, my nieces and nephews can do 100x more on their phones. Crazy.

Back then, an opportunity came up to bid on a series of television commercials for a regional grocery chain. The bid emphasized budget was an issue, but they needed to produce a large volume of content due to the different specials the chain ran weekly, sometimes even mixing it up for different locations.

The other producers and production houses that put in bids all talked about the quality of their tape decks and how fast they could churn out '4-5 spots' a week for the grocery chain due to the speed of their editors. They all also talked about the volume of industry awards they had won and how basically, they were the only ones who could handle the work being asked for.

Thinking about it, I realized the grocery folks could care less about tape formats or industry awards, and they wanted to sell food – they wanted to sell a ton of it! The answer to winning the bid wasn't to talk about the speed of my produced work, or even the production technology of the day – but to talk about the volume of work I could produce in the same amount of production time – **for less money!** Using the AVID, which transferred video footage to a hard drive (revolutionary at the time), that you could then organize into different folders or "bins," I could produce more commercials at scale. I submitted a proposal outlining how I could consistently churn out up to 12 spots a week for less budget than the other guys were proposing 4-5 spots a week. Not only that, but I could create an 'on-call' digital library of their most popular items. In time, I could lower their weekly production costs because I would get to the point where instead of having to shoot avocados that week with a hired video crew, I would already have them stored in my "digital vegetable library", hence saving them a ton of production expenses over time.

I won that bid. I gave them a solution that benefited them today, and in the future. I didn't talk about my resume, my awards, or how great my studio or techniques were. I focused on their problem and gave them a solution that went beyond what they were anticipating.

"IF YOU THINK YOU'RE TOO SMALL
TO HAVE AN IMPACT, TRY GOING
TO BED WITH A MOSQUITO IN THE ROOM."

-ANITA RODDICK

# WHY IT'S IMPORTANT TO DEVELOP YOUR PROSPECTING SKILLS

Developing strong prospecting and sales skills is essential for businesses of all sizes looking to grow and succeed in today's competitive market. But the reality is, prospecting can sometimes feel like a never-ending game of cat and mouse – you're constantly trying to track down new leads and close deals, while your competition is hot on your tail. That's where the power of strong prospecting skills comes in!

By focusing on improving these skills, businesses can not only increase their revenue, but also build strong, long-term relationships with customers and stand out from the competition. Think of it like a dating app – if you're the type of person who can hold an interesting conversation, make a good first impression, and follow up consistently, you're more likely to find a match (or in this case, a customer).

Another benefit of developing strong prospecting skills is the ability to enhance the reputation of the business. By consistently delivering high-quality products or services and effectively communicating the value of these offerings to potential customers, businesses can build a positive reputation in the marketplace. This can lead to increased trust and credibility, as well as the opportunity to attract new customers and partnerships. Imagine if your business was like that one friend who always shows up to a party with a six-pack of craft beer – pretty soon, everyone is going to want to hang out with you.

Investing in sales training and development can also lead to greater employee satisfaction within the sales team. By providing opportunities for employees to improve their skills and knowledge, businesses can foster a culture of continuous learning and improvement. This can lead to increased job satisfaction and retention rates, as well as improved performance and productivity within the sales team. If you want to keep your employees happy, give them the tools they need to succeed (and maybe a few snacks).

"NOTHING ON THE PLANET HAPPENS UNTIL SOMEONE SELLS SOMETHING."

-JACK WARKENTHIEN

# THE PROSPECTING CHALLENGE

Finding new prospects and sales opportunities is a crucial part of growing a successful business, but it can also be a challenging task. Here are some common challenges businesses face when trying to find new prospects and sales opportunities:

**Competition:**

In today's market, there is often a lot of competition for customers, and it can be difficult to stand out from the crowd. This can make it challenging to attract new prospects and close sales.

**Lack of resources:**

Finding new prospects and sales opportunities can be time-consuming and resource intensive. If a business doesn't have the necessary resources (e.g., personnel, budget, tools), it can be difficult to effectively pursue new leads and close deals.

**Lack of a clear target audience:**

It's important to have a clear understanding of who your target audience is and how to effectively reach them. If a business doesn't have a clear understanding of their ideal customer, it can be challenging to generate new leads and close sales.

**Limited access to decision-makers:**

In some cases, businesses may struggle to access decision-makers within a target company. This can make it difficult to pitch products or services and close deals.

**Limited budget for marketing and sales efforts:**

Marketing and sales efforts can be expensive, and businesses may not have the budget to pursue new leads or invest in sales training and development. This can make it challenging to generate new prospects and close deals.

**Lack of a strong brand:**

A strong brand can help businesses attract new prospects and close deals, but if a business lacks a strong brand, it can be challenging to stand out from the competition and generate new leads.

Marketing and sales can sometimes feel like a never-ending game of whack-a-mole – as soon as you solve one problem, another one pops up. It can be tough to stand out in a crowded market, especially when you're competing against companies with bigger budgets and more resources. But don't worry, there's hope!

To overcome these challenges, businesses need to focus on building a strong brand, developing a clear understanding of their target audience, and investing in marketing and sales efforts that effectively reach and engage potential customers. Dress for the job you want, not the job you have. In this case, that means creating a brand that reflects your company's values, mission, and unique selling points.

It can also be helpful to invest in sales training and development (like reading this book!), as well as tools and technologies that can help streamline the sales process and make it easier to generate new leads and close deals. Think of it like hiring a personal trainer – they'll help you get in shape and achieve your goals faster.

Finally, businesses can consider partnering with other companies or organizations to access new markets and expand their reach. Two heads are better than one. By partnering with other businesses, you can combine your resources and reach a wider audience.

So, don't let the challenges of marketing and sales get you down! With a strong brand, a clear understanding of your target audience, and a little bit of investment, you can overcome any obstacle and drive your business to success.

**Visit www.ProspectingHacks.com for free guides that will help you with your prospecting game plan.**

 **FROM THE FIELD**

For a while I had a salesperson that worked for me. He would run around the city trying to find new clients that wanted websites using my Godfather offer (more on that in a bit). The rules I gave my sales guy were he had to do the closing because I didn't have time, but if he HAD to pull me into the meeting, the prospect had better be ready to close, and I never want to go downtown. I hate going downtown.

On some rainy afternoon my sales guy calls me. "John, I've got this prospect, he's close to signing up for a $5,000 website, but I'm not sure if I can close him. Will you come with me to the next meeting?" Ugh. "Fine" I said. Guess where this meeting was... downtown. I'm not happy.

We go downtown, we go up to the 20th floor of some building and meet with this guy. Not only did he NOT sign up for the project, but he was nowhere near ready. I am not happy. We walk out of the office and my sales guy is apologetically just talking about anything. "There's a bar downstairs, let's grab a drink and figure this out." I don't even look at him. We get into the elevator, and I press the button for the 19th floor. He just looks at me.

I walk to the office that was under our prospects' office, read the name on the door and Google it. With a few more moments of research, I discover there is a large trade show coming up for them. I walk in their office, (with my sales guy walking behind me still trying to figure out what I'm up to), and ask to talk with Mr._____, "I'm here to talk about re-designing their new website for the show coming up." The gatekeeper says, "Ya know, they were just talking about that the other day, just a moment." A few moments go by and Mr. ____ walks out. I give him my Godfather elevator pitch and he invites us in. An hour later we (I) walk out with a check for $17,000 to redesign their online presence, as well as become their web agency for future web management.

I hit the button on the elevator. I look at my sales guy and say, "Now we can get a drink."

My sales guy was ready to just accept the negative reaction from the first meeting. He didn't give himself permission to do something about it.

He doesn't work for me anymore.

"HALF OF GETTING THERE IS HAVING THE CONFIDENCE TO SHOW UP, AND KEEP SHOWING UP."

-SOPHIA AMORUSO

# MAKE YOURSELF THE "GO-TO" EXPERT

## *"If you haven't created an online brand for yourself, you don't exist to your prospect."*

As a **Subject Matter Expert (S.M.E.)**, you are like a walking encyclopedia of knowledge in a specific field or subject. You can become an expert in anything, as long as you have a thorough understanding of the subject matter and can effectively communicate your knowledge to others. It was true yesterday, it's true today, and it will be true tomorrow - *Knowledge is power*!

In order to gain credibility and increase your chances of success in the professional world, it is important to establish yourself as an authority in your field. This can involve getting certified, continuing your education, defining your niche, making professional connections and nurturing your network, and building an online presence. If you want to succeed, you have to be a jack of all trades (or at least a master of one).

One way to gain credibility is to become certified in your field. This can involve earning a degree or obtaining a professional certification that demonstrates your knowledge and expertise. By getting certified, you can show potential customers that you are serious about your career and have the skills and knowledge to advise them on their business. If you want to be taken seriously, you have to put in the work. **Read that sentence again.**

Continuing your education is also crucial for building credibility as a subject matter expert. Industries are constantly evolving, and it is important to stay up-to-date with new developments, trends, and hot topics in your field. This can involve reading industry publications, attending events like workshops, webinars, and conferences, and staying informed about world news that may impact your field. By staying informed, you can demonstrate to your potential customer that you are a reliable source of information and can provide answers to their most pressing questions. *If you want to succeed, you have to keep learning*. Personally, I read 2-3 books a week about my industry. This is why I have had the success I have had in my field.

Defining your niche and creating a clear message are also important for building credibility as a subject matter expert. It is important to define who you are, what you do, and who you are serving so that you can effectively communicate your expertise to your audience. In addition to starting your own platforms, such as a website or blog, you can also pitch your expertise as a guest blogger or podcast guest, or collaborate with other industry professionals on events where you can share your knowledge with a wider audience. If you want to stand out, you have to find your niche.

Making professional connections and nurturing your network is also crucial for building credibility as a subject matter expert. You can start networking in your industry by commenting on LinkedIn updates, following industry leaders, joining professional groups and organizations, and attending networking events. By making connections and building relationships with others in your field, you can gain valuable insights, learn from experienced professionals, and increase your visibility within your industry. It's not what you know, it's who you know.

Building an online presence is *essential* for building credibility as a subject matter expert. This can involve creating a podcast, YouTube channel, LinkedIn profile, starting a blog or website, and sharing your expertise on social media. By building an online presence, you can showcase your skills and knowledge to a wider audience and increase your chances of being discovered by potential clients.

**Develop time management skills.** Time management is a crucial skill for an SME. With so many responsibilities, it's important to be able to prioritize and manage your time effectively.

**Establish yourself as a public authority in your field.** One way to do this is by setting up an informative and regularly updated website or blog. This will give you a platform to share your thoughts and opinions with your target audience.

**Utilize social media platforms.** Platforms such as YouTube and blogging sites are great ways to showcase your expertise and establish yourself as a thought leader.

**Plan your career accordingly.** If you work in an authoritative role such as management, it may be easier to be recognized as an SME. So, plan your career accordingly and choose roles that will help you become an SME in your field.

**Prioritize authenticity.** Finally, it's important to be authentic and true to yourself when trying to establish yourself as an SME. This will help you gain the trust and respect of your peers.

Following these strategies, you can establish yourself as an expert in your field and increase your chances of success in the professional world. **If you want to succeed, you have to put in the work, stay informed, find your niche, make connections, and build your online presence.** Don't worry, it's not as daunting as it sounds – just take it one step at a time, and before you know it, you'll be the go-to expert in your field!

"NEVER UNDERSELL YOURSELF UNLESS YOU WANT EVERYONE ELSE TO."

-ELAINE DUNDY

# IDENTIFY AND UNDERSTAND YOUR PROSPECT AVATAR

Identifying your ideal customer is a crucial step in the process of building and growing a successful business. By focusing on a specific group of customers who are most likely to benefit from and be interested in your products or services, you can create targeted marketing campaigns and tailor your offering to better meet the needs and preferences of this group.

### Define your target audience:

The first step in identifying your ideal customer is to define the characteristics of the people you want to reach. Consider factors such as age, gender, location, income, education level, and interests. You may also want to think about what motivates your target audience and what problem your product or service can help solve for them.

### Research your market:

To get a better understanding of your target audience, it's important to research your market. This can involve looking at industry reports, conducting surveys or focus groups, and analyzing data from your own customer base. This research will help you gather valuable insights about your target audience and determine how to effectively reach and engage them.

**Ask yourself these questions to make sure your avatar matches with your services and offers:**

- What is the online reputation of the prospect?
- What exactly do they do? Are they a good fit for your offerings?
- What is their mission?
- Are they stable financially?
- Who are the company's competitors?
- What are their differentiators?

It's also important to understand the decision-making process within the company you are targeting. Who is involved in making purchasing decisions? What are the key factors that influence their decision? Having this information can help you tailor your messaging and pitch to address their specific needs and concerns.

In addition to understanding the business and decision-making process, it's crucial to also have a clear understanding of your own product or service. What are the key features and benefits? How does it solve the problems or meet the needs of your ideal customer? Being able to clearly articulate the value of your offering can be a major factor in successfully converting a prospect into a customer.

It can also be helpful to identify potential objections that a prospect may have and be prepared to address them. This can help to overcome any barriers that may be preventing a company from considering your solution.

Having a clear understanding of your ideal customer and the value your product or service provides can be a key factor in successful B2B prospecting efforts. By doing your research and being prepared to address the needs and concerns of your target audience, you can effectively communicate the benefits of your offering and increase your chances of making a successful sale.

**Create buyer personas:**

Once you have a clear understanding of your target audience, it can be helpful to create detailed buyer personas. A buyer persona is a fictional representation of your ideal customer based on the research you have gathered. This can include information such as their demographics, goals, challenges, and how they prefer to receive information. Creating buyer personas can help you get a better sense of who your ideal customer is and how to effectively communicate with them.

By defining your target audience, conducting market research, and creating buyer personas you can reach and engage the right customers and build a loyal customer base.

Thorough research and a clear understanding of your ideal customer, the decision-making process, and the value of your product or service are key to conducting effective B2B prospecting efforts. By focusing on the needs of your target audience and being prepared to address their concerns, you can increase your chances of making successful sales. I can't stress enough, (and I do throughout this book), **SELL THE SOLUTION**, don't waste the customers time going on about your accomplishments, how successful your company is, or how many industry awards you have won. If someone is giving you their time on the phone or in person, in this day and age, they have already Googled you and your company and know everything they want to know. Don't waste their time, don't waste yours. Spend the precious opportunity they have given you finding a solution to a problem they have that you have the answer to.

**I ALWAYS CRUSH MY COMPETITION BECAUSE I MAKE SURE I KNOW EVERYTHING ABOUT MY PROSPECT AND MY SOLUTION BEFORE THE MEETING EVER HAPPENS! I WIN THE PITCH BEFORE THE PITCH HAPPENS!**

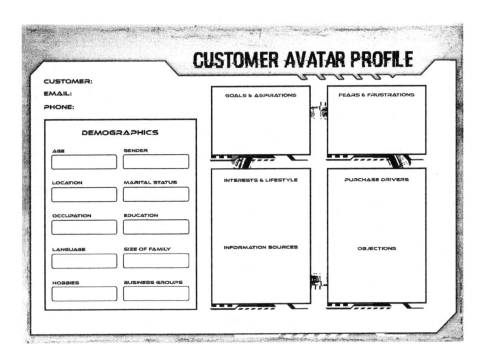

"THE ELEVATOR TO SUCCESS IS OUT OF ORDER.  YOU'LL HAVE TO USE THE STAIRS, ONE STEP AT A TIME."

-JOE GIRARD

# CREATE A "GODFATHER" OFFER

A "Godfather" offer is a high-value, irresistible offer that is designed to win over customers and drive sales. **It's important that your offer is seen as an "Aspirin" not a "Vitamin".** Your offer must have a sense of urgency that fixes the prospects headache, not just make them feel like they are living healthy.

**Here's a step-by-step guide to creating a Godfather offer for your sales prospecting:**

### Identify your target audience:

Before you can create an effective Godfather offer, you need to know who you're targeting. This means identifying the specific group of people who are most likely to be interested in your product or service. Consider factors like their age, income level, location, and interests when identifying your target audience.

### Determine the value of your product or service:

Next, you need to understand the value that your product or service provides to your target audience. What problems does it solve? How does it make their lives better? By understanding the value of your product or service, you can create an offer that is compelling and relevant to your prospects.

### Determine the price of your product or service:

Now that you understand the value of your product or service, it's time to determine the price. This will be the foundation of your Godfather offer. Be sure to consider the price of similar products or services in the market, as well as your own costs and profitability.

**Create a compelling offer:**

Now it's time to craft your Godfather offer. Make it generous and attractive by offering a significant discount or added value, such as a free trial or additional features. Be sure to clearly communicate the value of your offer to your prospect.

**Set a deadline for your offer:**

To create a sense of urgency, it's important to set a deadline for your Godfather offer. This will encourage your prospect to act quickly and make a decision.

**Make it easy for your prospect to accept your offer:**

Finally, make it easy for your prospect to say yes to your Godfather offer. This could mean providing multiple payment options, offering a risk-free trial, or making it easy for them to cancel if they're not satisfied.

If you go to OpenAI, https://openai.com/, and sign up for a free Chat GPT account, you can use AI to help you write the perfect Godfather offer with SEO keywords for your industry. Once your account is created, go to the prompt and type in: **Write a godfather offer for (your industry)**

Some *basic* examples of a "Godfather" offer:

1. Offer a significant discount on a product or service. If you're a small business owner looking to acquire a new customer or client, consider offering a significant discount on your product or service. For example, if you own a cafe, you could offer a

50% discount on a meal or a free dessert with the purchase of a drink.

2. Offer additional value or bonuses. In addition to offering a discount, you could also consider offering additional value or bonuses to your prospects. For example, if you own a fitness studio, you could offer a free personal training session or a month of unlimited classes with the purchase of a membership.

3. Offer a risk-free trial. Another way to create a Godfather offer for your small business is to offer a risk-free trial. This allows your prospects to try out your product or service without any risk, which can be a powerful incentive. For example, if you own an e-commerce store, you could offer a money-back guarantee or a free return policy to encourage people to make a purchase.

By following these steps, you can create a Godfather offer that is difficult for your sales prospects to refuse.

 **FROM THE FIELD**

I have spent my entire career in the media development business. I started in film, then video, then different new media formats like CD-Rom and DVD, then websites, then apps. In the media development business, formats aren't really too much of an issue when it comes to the project. Creating the content that goes on the format is where the art is. The content creation business is an exercise in patience. Everyone, from your client to your clients' nephew twice removed wants to give their two cents and be an art director. Whether you love it or not, at the end of the day the client is always right. I would guess to say that maybe 20% of the over 20,000 projects I have produced all over the world I have been proud of, the rest are what the client wanted.

I am not the only person in this business to experience this. Because of that, early on (like since media development was born), entities like ad agencies and freelance talent have always "nickel and dimed" clients every time they wanted to change something. This can be very expensive for the client. Realizing this early on in my career I saw that I had an opportunity to create a Godfather offer that would guarantee I would always (or close to it) win the project — ***"Unlimited changes for one flat turnkey price"***. That has always been my Godfather offer, and as predicted, it not only got me tons of business, but a reputation.

The volume of referrals I have received over the years, from all over the world, has been amazing. I'll do a project for a client, keep to my word, then they are at a party or something and someone there is complaining about how they had a terrible experience getting their website off the ground, my client overhears them and tells them about me. Two, maybe three times a year a client takes advantage of my offer and I get screwed over from a time perspective. But, compared to 75% margins I enjoy with the rest of the projects for the year, it's just a cost of doing business.

"A MARKETING PROFESSOR ASKED HIS STUDENTS,
"IF YOU WERE GOING TO OPEN A HOT DOG STAND,
AND YOU COULD ONLY HAVE ONE ADVANTAGE
OVER YOUR COMPETITORS... WHICH WOULD IT BE?"

"LOCATION!... QUALITY!...LOW PRICES!...BEST TASTE!"

THE STUDENTS JUST SAT THINKING UNTIL
ONE OF THEM ASKED, "WHICH ONE?".

THE PROFESSOR SMILED AND REPLIED,
"A STARVING CROWD."

-ALEX HORMOZI

# PERFECT YOUR ELEVATOR PITCH

An elevator pitch is a brief, persuasive speech that is designed to sell an idea or product in a short amount of time (typically the time it takes to ride an elevator). To perfect your elevator pitch, here are some steps you can follow:

### Identify the key benefits of your product or idea:

To persuade your audience, you need to clearly communicate the benefits of your product or idea. Think about what makes your offering unique and how it can solve a problem or meet a need for your audience.

### Keep it simple and concise:

An elevator pitch should be brief and to the point. Avoid using jargon or technical language that your audience may not understand, and focus on the key points that will grab their attention and persuade them to take action.

### Use storytelling to engage your audience:

A good story can help engage your audience and make your pitch more memorable. Consider incorporating a personal anecdote or case study into your pitch to illustrate the value of your product or idea.

### Practice, practice, practice:

To deliver a successful elevator pitch, you need to practice and rehearse it until it feels natural and polished. This will help you feel more confident and comfortable when delivering your pitch and allow you to make any necessary adjustments.

**Be prepared for objections:**

It's likely that you will encounter objections during your pitch, and it's important to be prepared to address these objections and keep the conversation moving forward. Consider potential objections ahead of time and have responses ready to address them.

Remember, to perfect your elevator pitch, you need to know your audience, identify the key benefits of your product or idea, keep it simple and concise, use storytelling to engage your audience, *practice*, and be prepared for objections. By following these steps, you can deliver a persuasive and effective elevator pitch that persuades your audience to take action.

 **FROM THE FIELD**

**Here is an example of one of my elevator pitches to a locksmith I met in the line at a grocery store, ended up getting $3,000 to make him a one-page website, then a retainer of $1500 a month.**

"Hi!, I'm John. What do you do? Ahh, Locksmith, that's very cool. Picking locks always fascinated me, I always wondered how you guys figured all that stuff out. My website firm specializes in getting locksmiths new customers so they can just focus on how to pick locks. We custom develop an online targeted traffic plan along with a new customer web page that features multiple touch points to gather new client information, that information is then sent directly to you as fast as possible via text message or tracked phone call. We guarantee new leads every month, all for one flat turnkey rate. How do you get new service calls now?"

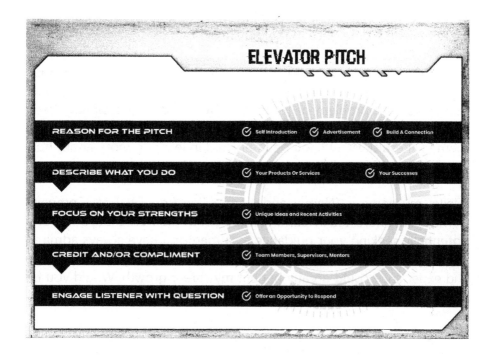

**Here are six examples of elevator pitches:**

"Hello, my name is [Name] and I am the founder of [Company]. We offer a platform that connects small business owners with affordable marketing services. Our team has a proven track record of helping businesses increase their online presence and drive more sales. Would you be interested in learning more about our services?"

"Hi, I'm [Name] and I have developed a new app called [App Name] that helps people track their daily water intake and provides personalized hydration reminders. This is especially useful for people who are active or have busy schedules. Are you interested in hearing more about how our app can help improve your overall health and wellness?"

"Hello, my name is [Name] and I am the CEO of [Company], a sustainable fashion brand that uses eco-friendly materials to create high-quality, stylish clothing. Our mission is to reduce the environmental impact of the fashion industry while still offering trendy and fashionable options.

Would you be interested in learning more about our brand and how we're making a difference in the industry?"

"Hi, my name is [Name] and I am a [Position Title] at [Company Name]. I am here to tell you about our innovative new product, [Product], that solves the problem of [Problem]. Our product has already been successfully implemented with [Example Customers] and has helped them to [Result]. Would you be interested in learning more about how [Product] could benefit your business as well?"

"Hello, my name is [Name] and I am a [Position Title] at [Company Name]. I am interested in learning more about the work that you do and potentially seeking your guidance as a mentor. I have always admired your expertise in [Area of Expertise] and believe that your knowledge and experience could greatly benefit my career growth. Would you be open to discussing a potential mentorship relationship with me?"

"Hi, my name is [Name] and I am a [Position Title] at [Company Name]. I am excited to tell you about the new project that I am working on, [Project], which aims to [Goal]. I have already gathered a strong team of experienced professionals and secured funding from [Investor]. I am confident that this project has the potential to [Potential Impact] and I would love the opportunity to discuss it with you further. Would you be interested in hearing more about [Project]?"

 **FROM THE FIELD**

Back in the late '90's, I found myself on the lot of Paramount Studios. How I got there is a different book. Walking around, I noticed that Paramount is actually a collection of different production companies, not just one big production studio. After a while, I wandered into a small café on the lot. Standing in line to order something I found myself talking to a wonderful lady named Leeza Gibbons. She was, at the time, one of the hosts of Entertainment Tonight (which was produced on the Paramount lot). While in line, she asked me about myself, and I shared with her a brief history of my professional and creative journey (my elevator pitch). By the time we both ordered, she had invited me to a dinner party at her house that night. I had been in Hollywood for one day at that point and I already got an invitation to an industry event (her dinner party), by having an elevator pitch ready for anyone who would listen. Go me!

That night, I met some amazing people. After dinner, we all kind of split off to different areas of the house. I found myself sitting by the pool sipping an Ole' Fashion. This guy walks up to me and asks if he can join me. Sitting down, he introduces himself as an executive producer for Mtv, (back then, they were still showing music videos). The moment he tells me who he is I readied my elevator pitch like I did with Leeza earlier that day. Before the night was over, he offered me a gig to help produce a new series they were starting with their sister network Vh-1 called 'Behind The Music'. I ended up spending the next 18 months interviewing rock stars and living a dream life in Hollywood... all because when the opportunity presented itself (in my case two opportunities on my very first day in Hollywood) I was ready with my elevator pitch.

 **AI TIP**

If you go to OpenAI, https://openai.com/, and sign up for a free Chat GPT account, you can use AI to help you write the perfect elevator pitch with SEO keywords for your industry. Once your account is created, go to the prompt and type in: **Write an elevator pitch for (your industry)**

"PRACTICE ISN'T THE THING YOU DO
ONCE YOU'RE GOOD.  IT'S THE THING
YOU DO THAT MAKES YOU GOOD."

-MALCOLM GLADWELL

# HOW TO HANDLE OBJECTIONS DURING YOUR PROSPECTING

Objections are a common and expected part of the sales process. While they can be frustrating, they also provide an opportunity for you to address any concerns or objections the customer has and help move the sales process forward.

**Here are some steps you can follow to handle objections during a sales meeting:**

### Listen carefully:

The first step in handling objections is to *listen carefully* to what the customer is saying. This will help you understand their concerns and objections and respond appropriately.

### Clarify the objection:

It's important to clarify the objection to ensure you fully understand it and can address it effectively. Ask questions to get more information and make sure you understand the customer's perspective. Don't get emotional or take things personally, you will only embarrass yourself, your company, and make the situation worse than it needs to be.

### Acknowledge and validate the objection:

It's important to acknowledge and validate the customer's concerns and objections, even if you don't agree with them. This can help build trust and credibility and show that you are listening and taking their needs into consideration.

**Respond with a solution:**

Once you have fully understood the objection, it's time to respond with a solution. This could involve providing additional information, addressing a concern, or offering a benefit or incentive to overcome the objection.

**Follow up:**

After addressing the objection, it's important to follow up to ensure that the customer is satisfied and that the objection has been fully addressed. This can involve checking in with the customer to see if they have any additional questions or concerns.

By following these steps, you can effectively handle objections during a sales meeting and move the sales process forward. It's important to remain calm and professional, and to focus on finding a solution rather than getting defensive or argumentative. By effectively handling objections, you can build trust and credibility with the customer and increase the likelihood of making a sale.

"IF PLAN 'A' FAILS, REMEMBER THAT YOU HAVE 25 MORE LETTERS."

-CHRIS GUILLEBEAU

# HOW TO GET PAST "GATE KEEPERS"

Cold outreach can be a daunting task for many salespeople, especially when it comes to getting past gatekeepers. These individuals, often receptionists or administrative assistants, are the first point of contact for potential customers and can make or break a sales call. The good news is that there are strategies and techniques that can be used to effectively navigate the gatekeeper and reach the decision-maker.

First and foremost, it is important to have a clear and concise message. The gatekeeper is likely to field a large number of calls as well as emails, and may not have the time or patience to listen to a long-winded introduction. Instead, be prepared with a brief and compelling pitch that can be delivered in 30 seconds or less. This should include the purpose of the cold outreach, the value proposition of the product or service, and a call to action.

Another key strategy is to be confident and assertive. Gatekeepers are often trained to screen cold outreach efforts and may be more likely to transfer a cold outreach email or even call if the caller sounds unsure or uncertain. Speak clearly and confidently and be prepared to ask for the decision-maker by name. It can also be helpful to have a reason for why the decision-maker should answer the email or take the call, such as a recent article or industry event that is relevant to their business.

It is also essential to be respectful and courteous when speaking with gatekeepers. Remember that they are individuals with their own busy schedules and responsibilities and may not be interested in being bothered by a cold outreach email or sales call. Showing respect and understanding can go a long way in building a positive relationship and potentially gaining access to the decision-maker.

Another technique that can be used to get past gatekeepers is to use a technique called "piggybacking." This involves finding a common connection or point of interest between the gatekeeper and the decision-maker and using it as a way to build a relationship. For example, if the gatekeeper is a fan of a particular sports team, the caller can mention that they are also a fan and use that as a way to initiate a conversation. This can help to establish a rapport and make it more likely that the call will be transferred.

Another effective strategy is to use a "hook" in the introduction. A hook is a unique and interesting fact or piece of information that can capture the gatekeeper's attention and make them more likely to transfer the cold outreach email or call. For example, if the caller is selling a new product that is environmentally friendly, they can mention that it is made from recycled materials and has a lower carbon footprint than other products on the market. This type of hook can be used to pique the gatekeeper's interest and make them more likely to transfer the call.

In addition to these strategies, it is also essential to be prepared and organized when making cold outreach attempts. This includes having a list of decision-makers, their contact information, and any relevant information about the company and industry. It can also be helpful to use a call script or guide that can help to keep the conversation on track and ensure that all key points are covered.

Another key aspect of cold outreach is to be persistent. It is important to remember that not every email or call will result in a sale, and that it may take several attempts to reach the decision-maker. It is essential to be persistent and not give up after one or two cold outreach attempts.

Getting past gatekeepers when making cold outreach attempts can be a challenging task, but it is not impossible. By using a clear and concise message, being confident and assertive, showing respect and understanding, using piggybacking, using a hook, being prepared and organized, and being persistent, you can increase your chances of reaching the decision-maker and closing the sale. Remember, gatekeepers are not the enemy, they are simply doing their job of screening calls. By approaching them with a friendly and professional demeanor, you can increase the likelihood of being transferred to the decision-maker. Keep in mind that it may take multiple attempts to reach the decision-maker, but by using these strategies and techniques, you can increase your chances of success. Remember to always be respectful, professional and persistent and you will be able to make your way to the decision-makers and close the deal.

 **FROM THE FIELD**

**How to get past the gate keeper when you are going door to door through an office building:**

1.  **Try Transparency - The "Pop In – Cold Call":**
    **Gate Keeper:** Hi, may I help you?
    **You:** Hi! I was just next door, saw your office and realized you guys are a client I have been trying to land for a while, so I just thought I would do the "pop in-cold call" to see if I could leave some information or maybe talk to someone for just a moment. Bad idea? Should I just go?
    **Gate Keeper:** Ha Ha Ha.... It's fine.
    **You:** Really? That's very cool of you.... Can I try my pitch on you first, let me know if it might work?
    **Gate Keeper:** Ha, ya, go ahead.

2.  **Become "One of Them":**
    "Instead of saying 'I want to show David how to increase sales at his used car lot', try using industry-specific language and references, such as 'Bob at TX Auto suggested I reach out to you to schedule a meeting with David. I can help move inventory for his dealership."

3. **Do your homework:**

   Research the gatekeeper ahead of time by checking out their LinkedIn profile. See if they have experience with similar products or services to yours and look up their previous companies. Use this information to show that you've done your research and can bring up positive experiences or avoid negative ones. This will demonstrate that you value their time and are not there to waste it.

"YOUR FIRST TEN WORDS ARE MORE
IMPORTANT THAN YOUR NEXT
TEN THOUSAND."

-ELMER WHEELER

 # LET'S GET PROSPECT HACKING

It's time to put those skills to work and start finding those dream customers! Remember, finding new clients is not only crucial for the success of your business, but it's also a chance to make a positive impact on the world. **As promised on the cover of this book, here are some of my favorite ways to find new prospects, all of which I have personally used to great success without having to resort to buying ads or cold calling.**

### Network and build relationships:

Don't be shy! Attend industry events, join professional organizations, and make connections through social media and online platforms. Building relationships can not only help you find new clients, but it can also lead to valuable collaborations and opportunities for growth.

### Utilize online marketing:

In today's digital age, online marketing is a powerful tool for reaching new clients. Use social media, email marketing, and online advertising to showcase your products or services and reach potential customers.

### Offer value:

In order to attract new clients, it's important to offer value and demonstrate the benefits of working with your business. This can include offering free resources, such as ebooks or webinars, or providing excellent customer service to show your dedication to meeting the needs of your clients. But always remember to lead with a **"Solution**

**First"** approach, then if there is interest you can get into the weeds of the company.

## Collaborate with complementary businesses:

Partnering with businesses that offer complementary products or  services can be a great way to find new clients. Consider cross-promoting each other's offerings or collaborating on joint ventures to reach a wider audience.

## Follow up and stay in touch:

Once you have made initial contact with a potential client, it's important to follow up and stay in touch. Keep them informed about your products or services and be available to answer any questions or concerns they may have.

Finding new clients requires persistence and a clear strategy. Don't be afraid to take risks and try new approaches, and always be open to learning and improving. And remember, with hard work and determination, you can find the success you deserve and make a positive impact on the world.

## Go out there and make that money!

**Visit** www.ProspectingHacks.com **for free guides that will help you with your prospecting game plan.**

"THE BIGGEST HUMAN TEMPTATION IS TO SETTLE FOR TOO LITTLE."

-THOMAS MERTON

# ONLINE PROSPECTING

# CREATE AN EMAIL LIST OF POTENTIAL CLIENTS/CUSTOMERS

Before you can get started using *SOME* of the Prospecting Hacks outlined in this book, you need to get a contact list of your prospects – physical addresses, email addresses, phone numbers, etc. This list is based on the exercise you did a couple of chapters back, "Identify and Understand Your Prospect Avatar".

Email lists can be a powerful tool for sales prospecting, as they allow businesses to reach a targeted audience and generate leads. By collecting email addresses from potential customers and building a list, businesses can send targeted campaigns to a specific group of people who have expressed interest in their products or services.

However, using an email list for sales prospecting requires a strategic approach. Simply sending mass emails to a list of random addresses is unlikely to be effective and may even lead to complaints or unsubscribes. Here are some best practices for using an email list for sales prospecting:

**Build your list organically:**

The best way to build an email list for sales prospecting is to collect email addresses from people who are genuinely interested in your products or services. This can be done through sign-up forms on your website or social media platforms, or by offering something of value (such as a free guide or webinar) in exchange for an email address. Avoid purchasing lists or adding people to your list without their consent, as this can lead to low engagement and damage your reputation.

**Segment your list:**

Once you have a list of email addresses, it's important to segment it based on common characteristics or interests. This allows you to tailor your messaging and send targeted campaigns to specific groups of people. For example, you might segment your list based on location, industry, or the products or services they are interested in.

**Personalize your emails:**

Personalized emails are more likely to be opened and read, so it's important to customize your messaging for each segment of your list. This can involve using the recipient's name in the subject line or body of the email, or addressing their specific interests or needs. Video email is also great for this! (more on that later).

**Use an email marketing platform:**

An email marketing platform can make it easier to manage your email list and create targeted campaigns. These platforms often come with features such as templates, scheduling, and analytics, which can help you streamline your email marketing efforts.

When it comes to email marketing service providers, Mailchimp, https://mailchimp.com/, ActiveCampaign, https://www.activecampaign.com/ and GetResponse, https://www.getresponse.com/, are three of the most popular options. Each of these platforms has its own set of features and pricing plans, making it difficult to determine which one is the best fit for your business.

One of the main differences between these three platforms is the ease of use. According to some users, Mailchimp is the most user-friendly of the three, with an intuitive interface and a straightforward sign-up process. ActiveCampaign and GetResponse also have relatively easy-to-use interfaces, but some users have found them to be slightly more complex than Mailchimp.

All three platforms – Mailchimp, ActiveCampaign, and GetResponse – offer a range of features and pricing plans that make them suitable for different businesses. Mailchimp is generally regarded as the most user-friendly platform, with good-looking templates and a free plan that allows you to send emails to up to 2,000 subscribers. GetResponse also has a free plan and a wide range of templates, but the designs may not be as visually appealing as those offered by Mailchimp. ActiveCampaign has a slightly lower starting price than the other two platforms and offers a sales CRM as a feature, but some users have found the templates to be less visually appealing. Ultimately, the best choice for your business will depend on your specific needs and budget.

**Test and optimize:**

It's important to regularly test and optimize your email campaigns to see what works and what doesn't. This can involve A/B testing subject lines, testing different templates or messaging, and analyzing your results to see what leads to the highest engagement and conversions.

By following these best practices, businesses can effectively use an email list for sales prospecting and generate leads. However, it's important to remember that email marketing is just one piece of the puzzle. To be successful in sales prospecting, businesses should also focus on building a strong brand, developing a clear understanding of their target audience, and investing in marketing and sales efforts that effectively reach and engage potential customers.

In addition, it's important to be mindful of best practices for email marketing and respect the privacy of your recipients. This includes following email marketing laws (such as the CAN-SPAM Act in the United States), providing an opt-out option for recipients who no longer want to receive emails from you, and being transparent about how you will use their email address.

**There are various methods and tools that can be used to find email addresses on the web for sales prospects.**

**Use a familiar email format:**

If you have the email address of someone who works at the same company as your lead, try using the same pattern. For example, if John Smith's email address is j.smith@xyzcompany.com, Jane Doe's might be j.doe@xyzcompany.com.

**Use email finder tools:**

Email finder tools are used to collect the email addresses of leads based on their personal information such as their name, social media profile, website, company name, and so on. These tools analyze webpages and collect every email address that has been posted on the internet. Many of these tools can enable you to perform both simple and advanced searches. Be mindful of people's privacy though. You don't want to create a reputation of being a spammer. I would suggest using the services below as a last resort compared to growing an online relationship organically with a potential prospect.

**Here is a list of platforms where you can find contact info for your avatar:**

| | |
|---|---|
| Hunter.io | https://hunter.io/ |
| Apollo.io | https://www.apollo.io/ |
| Lusha | https://www.lusha.com/ |
| Uplead | https://www.uplead.com/ |
| Find That Lead | https://findthatlead.com/en |
| D7LeadFinder | https://d7leadfinder.com/ |
| Swordfish AI | https://swordfish.ai/ |
| SellHack | https://sellhack.com/ |

**Search for the person's social media profiles:**

Many people list their email addresses on their social media profiles, especially on LinkedIn. You can search for the person's profile on LinkedIn and try to find their email address there.

**Use public directories:**

There are several public directories available on the internet that list email addresses. These directories can be searched using the person's name, company name, or job title.

**Use the company's website:**

If you are trying to contact someone from a specific company, you can try searching for their email address on the company's website. Many companies list their employees' email addresses on their website, either on the contact page or on the employee's personal profile page.

**Use the person's personal website:**

If the person has a personal website, you may be able to find their email address there. Many people list their email addresses on their personal websites in order to make it easy for others to contact them.

**Email Verification:**

When you send an email, it is transmitted from your email server to the email server of the recipient, which stores the email address you are trying to contact. If the email address is invalid or no longer in use, the email will bounce back. This can be a problem for businesses, as a high number of bounced emails from a single account or IP address can make it appear as if you are sending spam. As a result, other mail servers may label your emails as spam and send them to the recipient's trash or spam folder, or even blacklist your email address. To avoid these issues, it is important to verify that the emails you are sending to are active and in use.

**Email Verification Platforms:**

**Never Bounce**        https://neverbounce.com/
**Bulk Email Checker**  https://www.bulkemailchecker.com/

When using a combination of these techniques and tools, you should be able to find email addresses for your sales prospects on the web. It is important to be persistent and to try multiple methods, as it may take some time to find the correct email address. It is also important to be respectful of people's privacy and to only use their email addresses for legitimate business purposes.

By using an email list for sales prospecting and following best practices, businesses can effectively reach their target audience and generate leads. With a little bit of strategy and planning, email lists can be a powerful tool for driving sales and growth for businesses of all sizes.

**Visit** www.ProspectingHacks.com **for free guides that will help you with your prospecting game plan.**

"ALL THE FANCY FOOTWORK IS GREAT.
BUT IF YOU WANT TO SCORE,
YOU HAVE TO SHOOT."

-ERIC COLE

# COLD EMAIL PROSPECTING

Cold email can be an effective tool for sales prospecting if used correctly.

### Research your target audience:

It is important to thoroughly research your target audience before sending a cold email. This includes finding the right email addresses, understanding their needs and preferences, and identifying any potential pain points or challenges they may be facing. This will allow you to craft a more targeted and personalized email that is more likely to resonate with your audience. Understand the prospects pain. ***Offer them an "Aspirin" not a "Vitamin"!***

### Keep the email brief:

As mentioned earlier, it is important to keep your cold email short and to the point. Aim for a maximum of 100 words, and focus on highlighting the benefits of your product or service, rather than listing all of its features.

### Personalize the email:

Personalization can be an effective way to increase the chances of your cold email being read and responded to. Use the recipient's name, mention any common connections you may have, or reference a specific pain point that your product or service can help solve.

### End with a clear call-to-action:

It is important to end your cold email with a clear call-to-action that tells the recipient what you want them to do next. This could be scheduling a demo or consultation, signing up for a free trial, or simply requesting a reply. Make it easy for the recipient to take the next step by providing a clear and simple way for them to do so.

**Create a compelling subject line:**

The subject line of your cold email is the first thing that your recipient will see, so it is important to make it catchy and attention-grabbing. A strong subject line should be concise, informative, and relevant to the recipient. Avoid using spammy or gimmicky language, as this can decrease the chances of your email being opened and read.

**Here are some tips and examples of cold email subject lines that sales prospectors can use to increase the chances of their emails being read:**

**Keep it short:**

Keeping your cold email subject lines short is one of the best things you can do to ensure high open rates. A short, to-the-point subject line is easier for the recipient to quickly understand and is more likely to pique their curiosity. Examples of short subject lines include:

"Quick question about your product"
"Introducing our new service"
"Special offer for your company"

**Make an effort to be useful:**

Subject lines that offer value or are useful to the recipient are more likely to be opened. Examples of useful subject lines include:

"Improve your sales process with our tool"
"Free resource for small business owners"
"Expert advice on increasing website traffic"

**Use humor:**

Subject lines that are humorous can catch the recipient's attention and make your email stand out. However, be careful not to overdo it or come across as inappropriate. Examples of humorous subject lines include:

"Are you tired of boring subject lines?"
"Why settle for mediocre email subject lines?"
"Why hello there, gorgeous subject line"

**Be opinionated:**

Subject lines that take a strong stance or express an opinion can be effective in grabbing the recipient's attention. Just make sure to stay respectful and professional. Examples of opinionated subject lines include:

"Why your company needs our product"
"The truth about [industry trend]"
"Why [competitor's product] falls short"

**Use a sense of urgency:**

Subject lines that create a sense of urgency can encourage the recipient to open and read your email sooner rather than later. However, be careful not to use this tactic too often or it may lose its effectiveness. Examples of urgent subject lines include:

"Limited time offer: 50% off our product"
"Don't miss out on this opportunity"
"Act fast: special pricing ends tomorrow"

**Personalize at scale:**

Use personalized subject lines to increase the chances of your email being read. This can be as simple as including the recipient's name or company in the subject line.

Examples of personalized subject lines include:

"John, a quick question about your business"
"Hello [Company], introducing our new product"
"Personalized subject line for [Recipient]"

Following these tips and using the provided examples, sales prospectors can craft effective cold email subject lines that will increase the chances of their emails being read.

If you go to OpenAI, https://openai.com/, and sign up for a free Chat GPT account, you can use AI to help you write the perfect subject line using keywords for your industry. Once your account is created, go to the prompt and type in: **Write "x" amount of email subject lines about "x", "x", and "x"**

**Using Email Sales Funnels:**

Email marketing funnels are a powerful tool for businesses looking to generate leads and convert them into customers. **Here's a step-by-step guide on how to design an effective email marketing funnel:**

1. Define your audience: Before you start creating your email marketing funnel, it's important to define your target audience. Determine the demographics, pain points, and buying habits of your ideal customer. This information will help you create more targeted and effective emails.
2. Build your email list: Once you have defined your target audience, you need to start building your email list. There are various ways to do this, such as offering a lead magnet, such as an e-book or webinar, in exchange for contact information.
3. Create an attention-grabbing lead magnet: Your lead magnet should be something that your target audience is interested in, such as an e-book, webinar, or checklist. It should be something

that provides value and addresses a specific pain point of your target audience.

4. Create a landing page: Once you have your lead magnet, you need to create a landing page where people can opt-in to your email list. This page should have a clear call-to-action, such as "Download our e-book now" or "Sign up for our webinar."

5. Send a welcome email: Once someone opts-in to your email list, send them a welcome email. This email should thank them for signing up and give them more information about what they can expect from your emails.

6. Send a series of follow-up emails: After the welcome email, you should start sending a series of follow-up emails. These emails should provide more value, such as tips and tricks, and should also include a clear call-to-action, such as scheduling a consultation or purchasing a product.

7. Create a sales email: Once you've provided value and built trust with your follow-up emails, it's time to create a sales email. This email should clearly communicate the benefits of your product or service, and should include a clear call-to-action, such as "Buy now" or "Schedule a consultation."

8. Set up automation: To make the most of your email marketing funnel, set up automation so that the right emails are sent to the right people at the right time. For example, you can set up an automation to send the welcome email immediately after someone opts-in, and another automation to send the follow-up emails at specific intervals.

9. Use split testing: To ensure that your email marketing funnel is as effective as possible, use split testing to test different elements, such as subject lines, email content, and calls-to-action. This will help you determine what works best and make adjustments accordingly.

10. Analyze your results: Finally, it's important to analyze your results and make adjustments as needed. Look at your open rates, click-through rates, and conversion rates, and use this information to optimize your email marketing funnel and improve its effectiveness.

In addition to the above steps, you can also include other techniques like A/B testing, segmenting your list based on user behavior, etc. Incorporating different technologies like Email Service Providers (ESP), Marketing Automation Platforms (MAP) to track user behavior and trigger specific actions, can help in scaling the process and make it more effective.

By thoroughly researching your target audience, **understanding their pain**, crafting a compelling subject line, keeping the email brief, personalizing the message, and ending with a clear call-to-action, you can increase the chances of your cold email being read and responded to. By using cold email as part of a wider sales prospecting strategy, you can generate leads and ultimately drive more sales for your business. However, it is important to remember to always follow best practices for cold emailing, including obtaining permission from the recipient before sending the email and respecting their privacy and preferences.

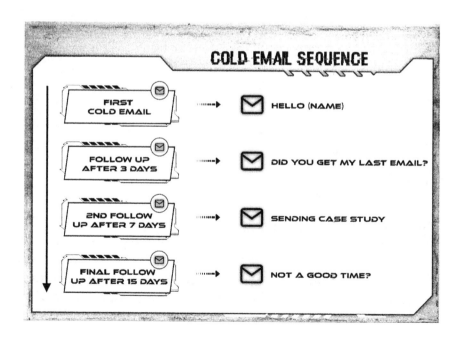

**Sample Cold Email:**

Dear [Prospect],

I hope this email finds you well. I recently came across your company's website and was impressed by the innovative products you offer. As the owner of [Your Company], we specialize in [Your Product/Service] and have helped numerous businesses like yours [Insert Benefits/Results- **How you fix their pain**].

I believe our [Product/Service] could greatly benefit your company and would love the opportunity to discuss this further with you. Could we schedule a brief call to discuss how we can help you achieve your business goals?

Thank you for considering my request. I look forward to speaking with you.

Best regards, [Your Name]

P.S. [Include a relevant success story or testimonial from a previous customer]

 **AI TIP**

If you go to OpenAI, https://openai.com/, and sign up for a free Chat GPT account, you can use AI to help you write the perfect cold email sales letters using keywords for your industry. Once your account is created, go to the prompt and type in: **Write a cold email sales letter addressed to a CEO featuring benefits of (your product or service)**

> "I'D RATHER REGRET THE THINGS
> I'VE DONE THAN REGRET THE THINGS
> I HAVEN'T DONE."
>
> -LUCILLE BALL

# VIDEO EMAIL PROSPECTING

Video email, sometimes called email video or video in email, is a way to include videos directly in the body of an email. An animated GIF file plays in the body of the email, the recipient clicks the animated GIF and it takest them to a web page that has your video along with links to your website, product pages, or even other videos!

In the past, video email providers have been available since the early-to-mid 2000s, but in recent years it has become more popular as a medium for email marketing. This is due to advances in technology, and it is often used to increase engagement rates. Many companies use video email to show off their brand, send newsletters, and announce events, products, or launches.

Video can help you send outreach emails more quickly and effectively. Here's why: Sales reps often spend a significant portion of their time, 21%, writing emails. By using video, you can save time in a few ways. You can record a short video instead of writing a lengthy message, or you can add a pre-recorded video to an email to add impact. Either way, video messages can be a big time-saver.

***Video can help improve the performance of your outreach emails in a number of ways:***

**Increase open rates:**

Sales teams that use video see a 16% increase in open rates, according to SalesLoft.

**Get more replies:**

Sales teams that use video receive 26% more replies, according to SalesLoft.

**Achieve higher click-through rates:**

Emails that contain video have 4 times the click-through rate of emails without video, according to Inside Sales.

**Close more deals:**

Webcams are used 41% more often in closed deals compared to lost deals, according to Gong.

**Gain a competitive advantage:**

Only 43.8% of sales teams currently use video in their prospecting strategy, according to Inside Sales. This means that by using video, you can differentiate yourself from your competitors.

Video can be useful not just for initial outreach, but also for follow-up communication. Sales reps know that timing is critical, and research shows that reps who reach out to leads within an hour are seven times more likely to have meaningful conversations with decision-makers. Video can help with this by providing real-time notifications when prospects have watched your videos, allowing you to follow up at the right moment.

**There are several situations in which video prospecting can be particularly effective:**

**Sending cold outreach:**

If you're new to video prospecting, recording and sharing a webcam or selfie-style video can be a way to stand out from traditional text-based cold emails.

**Reconnecting with a prospect:**

Sending a video message can be a good way to revisit a conversation with a prospect that has gone cold.

**Leveraging recent news to connect with an account:**

If a prospect's company has recently secured funding or had other exciting news, you can use this as an opportunity to reach out and congratulate them with a video message. This personalized video can help you stand out and explain how your solution could be a good fit at this transitional time.

**Prospecting from one-to-many:**

While personalized video is often the most effective way to connect with prospects, it's not always necessary. You can create a personalized video message at the account level, build a library of non-personalized video messages that answer frequently asked questions, or use a generic video response to inbound inquiries.

**Highlighting marketing content:**

If your marketing team has released a report or customer story that might be relevant to a prospect, consider sending a recorded screen-share video that walks them through the most relevant parts of the content.

**Keep a folder of pre-produced prospecting videos:**

To save time and scale your video prospecting efforts, you can leverage a folder of pre-recorded videos. This can include videos that you have recorded in advance to answer common questions or run through a demo script, as well as marketing-created videos like explainers and demos. By keeping these videos handy in a library, you can easily send them out whenever you need them, rather than having to record a new video every time. This can help you be more efficient in your prospecting efforts and allow you to focus on other tasks.

Ultimately, the best use of video in your prospecting strategy will depend on your process, business, and prospective customers. It can be helpful to test video at different points in your sales cadences to see where it works best.

***Creating prospecting videos is simple and can be more effective and efficient than other methods.***

**Here are the steps you can follow:**

**Choose the right timing:**

Before you start making your video, think about where it fits in your sales prospecting strategy. Will it be your initial outreach, a follow-up, or a last-ditch effort? Knowing this will help you decide what type of video to make and what to include in the script.

**Research your prospect:**

As with any effective outreach tactic, you need to know your prospect before you send them a video. Find out their job title, role in the organization, responsibilities, challenges, and pain points. This will help you craft a pitch that demonstrates how your solution can help them.

**Decide on the type of video to use:**

There are four different types of sales videos: webcam, screen share, playlist, and FAQ video. Each is best suited to different situations. For example, webcam videos are good for introducing yourself and building relationships, while screen share videos are good for explaining or walking through something.

**Write your script:**

If you already have a phone script or talking points, you can adapt them for video. If not, you can use a simple framework to structure your script. Start with an introduction, followed by a description of your value proposition, the purpose of your outreach, next steps and a call to action, and a "thank-you."

**Record your video message:**

This might feel intimidating at first but remember that small imperfections are what people often love most about personalized videos. If you're nervous, you can practice and follow some basic video production tips, like using the best lighting and sound available, and choosing your recording location carefully.

**Keep your video emails short:**

It's important to keep your prospecting videos short, as this shows respect for the prospect's time and increases the chances that they will watch the entire video. Cold outreach videos should generally be around 30 seconds to 60 seconds long. This means you should focus on the most important aspects of your message and eliminate any unnecessary content. According to research from the Video in Business Benchmark Report, while 54% of people will watch a video all the way through, regardless of length, over 60% will stay until the end if the video is less than 60 seconds long. By keeping your videos concise, you can increase the chances that your prospects will watch and engage with your content.

**Choose an attention-grabbing thumbnail:**

Your video will be more effective if it gets clicked on, so choose a thumbnail (animated GIF) that will catch your prospect's eye.

**Get creative with your video messages:**

Videos that are creative and out-of-the-box tend to be the most attention-grabbing and often get the best reactions from prospects. These types of videos can be especially effective in getting prospects to reply. By doing something unexpected and unique, you can differentiate yourself from other sales reps and capture your prospect's attention.

**Follow up with additional emails:**

After the first email, follow up with additional emails that continue to provide value and build a relationship with your prospect. These emails can include relevant industry news, case studies, or other information that aligns with their interests and needs.

**Use multiple forms of communication:**

In addition to emails, consider using other forms of communication such as phone calls, text messages, and social media to reach out to your prospect and increase the chances of getting a response.

**Close the sale:**

Once you've established a relationship and provided value to your prospect, it's time to close the sale. Use the information you've gathered about their needs and interests to tailor your sales pitch and address any objections they may have.

**Follow up after the sale:**

Even after the sale is closed, continue to follow up with your prospect to ensure they are satisfied with their purchase and to identify any potential upsell opportunities.

Using video in your email prospecting can increase the chances of getting a response and ultimately closing the sale. By personalizing the video message, following up with additional forms of communication, and providing value throughout, you are establishing yourself as a differentiator to your prospective customer.

# VIDEO EMAIL SEQUENCE

## AFTER HOURS

"Hello, (name) here. Thank you for reaching out to (dealership name). Unfortunately, we are currently closed but one of our sales consultants will be in touch with you as soon as we return. We are eager to assist you in your vehicle purchase."

## FIRST RESPONSE

"Hello, my name is (name) and I am the Sales Manager at (dealership name). I wanted to introduce myself and express my gratitude for considering us during your vehicle search. Our dealership has been serving the (city/town) community for (number) years, and we are excited to assist you in finding the perfect vehicle for your needs. You can contact me directly at (phone number) or by calling the dealership at (phone number). We look forward to welcoming you to our dealership soon."

## DAY 3,5,7 FOLLOW UP

"Hello, my name is (name) and I am the General Manager at (dealership name). I wanted to personally reach out to you to offer my assistance. I want to make sure you have received all the information you need regarding your recent inquiry. If there is anything my team or I can do to assist you, please do not hesitate to contact us at (phone number). We are here to help you in any way we can. Thank you and we look forward to speaking with you soon."

# VIDEO EMAIL SEQUENCE

## APPOINTMENT CONFIRMATION

"Hello, this is (name), General Manager at (dealership name). I wanted to confirm your appointment for today. Your vehicle is all set, gassed up, and ready for you! If you have any questions before your visit, please don't hesitate to call us. We are excited to see you soon!"

## UNSOLD SHOWROOM VISIT

"Hello, this is (name), General Manager at (dealership name). I wanted to thank you for your recent visit to our store and assure you that you are in good hands with your sales representative. If there is anything I can do to make your purchasing experience smoother, please don't hesitate to reach out to me. We are dedicated to assisting you in finding your perfect vehicle and look forward to helping you."

## SOLD VEHICLE THANK YOU

"Hello, this is (name), the General Manager at (dealership name). I wanted to personally thank you for your business and congratulate you on the purchase of your new vehicle! I hope you had a positive experience during your visit. We will continue to provide excellent service for you and your vehicle when you come in for maintenance. Thank you again for choosing our dealership. Have a great day!"

# FROM THE FIELD

I use a lot of video email to sing happy birthday to my clients (or prospects). They love it! One, they love someone remembered their birthday, and two, I'm not a good singer! So, they appreciate the effort.

 **AI TIP**

If you go to OpenAI, https://openai.com/, and sign up for a free Chat GPT account, you can use AI to help you write the perfect video email script using keywords for your industry. Once your account is created, go to the prompt and type in: **Write a video script sales letter addressed to a CEO featuring benefits of (your product or service)**

Also use Chat GPT to create a great subject line for your video email that the prospect will want to open. It's important for video email to start the subject line with "Video:_____" . Statistically, emails that have the word "video" in the subject get more opens.

**There are many ways you can make your prospecting videos more personalized and engaging.**

**Some simple ideas include:**

- Hold up a sign with their name on it so they can instantly see it's a personal video.
- Holding up a product from the prospect's company (if they make physical products)
- Aligning yourself with something the prospect is interested in, such as wearing a jersey from their favorite sports team

- Wishing them a happy birthday, holiday, or other occasion with a prop. When I send birthday video emails to clients I sing to them, I always get feedback how I made their day.

You can also get more creative with your video, such as wearing a costume, changing locations, or scripting a story. For example, one rep dressed up as Superman, while another recreated a scene from *Glen Garry Glen Ross*. These more elaborate approaches can be effective but be sure to test different strategies to see what works best for your business.

**Video Testimonials: Let your clients tell your prospective clients how great you are!**

Including video testimonials in your videos can help you build trust with your prospects and demonstrate that you are a legitimate business that knows what you're talking about. Instead of boasting about your own accomplishments, which can come across as arrogant, you can let your previous clients speak on your behalf.

By using video testimonials, you can earn credibility points and show your prospects that you have a track record of satisfied customers. The video email platforms I recommend below all have a feature that allows a recipient to reply to your video email. Simply make a video requesting a video testimonial, send it to your client and ask them to just 'reply with video'. They don't need to download anything or have special software. Takes a moment of their time and rewards you forever with a great video testimonial!

Video prospecting is an increasingly important tool for generating leads and conversions. To make the most of it, you need to follow best practices. This includes knowing your target audience, choosing the appropriate video format, including a strong call to action, using a catchy thumbnail, and featuring testimonials. You should also track your videos' performance and make adjustments as needed to improve your campaigns. With these tips in mind, and by combining your own creativity with a great product, your business can achieve success through video prospecting.

## Email Before You Video Email:

If you are doing cold email, and you want to maybe save some time as well as narrow down who is truly interested in what you are selling before you spend time making a bunch of videos, try sending an email before a video email. This hack works almost 100% of the time.

## Here's how it works:

Write a short regular email to the prospect, asking if they would like to see a video about "x".

> Hello (name)
>
> I made a video about (x) that I wanted to share with you because I think my company (x) can help you with (x).
>
> Would you like to see the video?
>
> Sincerely,
>
> (name)

You can do different versions, longer, or maybe make it more like you are taking a survey, but the idea is if they respond you've just turned a cold prospect into a warm lead!

## My favorite video email services are:

| | |
|---|---|
| Dubb | www.dubb.com |
| BombBomb | www.bombbomb.com |
| Vidyard | www.vidyard.com |
| Hippo | www.hippovideo.io |

"REMEMBER, THE UNIVERSAL LANGUAGE IS NOT TEXTED, EMAILED, OR SPOKEN. IT IS FELT."

-ANGELA AHRENDTS

# CREATE AN INDUSTRY NEWSLETTER

Having a newsletter for your business can be a powerful tool for increasing prospecting and driving growth and success for your business. Here are just a few of the ways that a newsletter can help you achieve these goals:

## Targeted content:

By creating a newsletter that is targeted to your specific audience, you can deliver content that is relevant and valuable to them. This can help attract new leads and potential customers, as well as improve customer loyalty and retention.

## Personalization:

With a newsletter, you can personalize your content and messages to appeal to different segments of your audience. By segmenting your email list and tailoring your content to specific groups, you can increase the chances of making a successful sale.

## Call-to-action:

By including a call-to-action in your newsletter, you can encourage your audience to take a specific action, such as visiting your website, filling out a form, or making a purchase. This can help increase the chances of generating new leads and closing sales.

## Market leadership:

By consistently publishing high-quality content that provides value to your audience, you can establish yourself as a thought leader in your field and increase your credibility and authority. This can help increase your reputation as a market leader and attract new leads and potential customers.

**Enhanced design:**

By investing in an eye-catching and professional design for your newsletter, you can improve the overall appearance and appeal of your content. This can help increase your credibility and authority, as well as make your newsletter more engaging and memorable for your audience.

Creating a newsletter for your business can be a powerful tool for increasing prospecting and driving growth and success for your business. By targeting your content, personalizing your messages, including a call-to-action, establishing yourself as a market leader, and enhancing the design of your newsletter, you can increase the chances of generating new leads and closing sales.

My two favorite platforms for creating newsletters are Substack (https://substack.com/) and Ghost (https://ghost.org/). Both have their pros and cons. I outlined a few differences below, but in my experience the easiest to use is Substack.

One major difference between Substack and Ghost is the type of platform they are. Substack is a hosted platform for creators to send newsletters, blog, and publish podcasts. This means that you don't have to install anything on your own server or web host in order to use it. Ghost, on the other hand, is an open-source publishing platform that you can install on your own server or web host. This means that you have more control over the platform and can customize it to your liking, but you'll also have to take care of the technical aspects of running it.

One important difference between Substack and Ghost is the level of customization they offer. Substack has a basic text editor that you can use to create your newsletters, but it doesn't offer many options for customizing the design or layout of your newsletters. Ghost, on the other hand, has a more dynamic editor that allows you to custom design your website and newsletters. This means you have more control over the look and feel of your content on Ghost.

Another factor to consider is cost. Substack charges $50 for a custom domain, while Ghost offers a free custom domain. This means that if you want to use your own domain name with Substack, you'll have to pay an additional fee.

It's worth noting that Ghost is a non-profit, open-source platform, while Substack is a for-profit company. Ghost was founded in 2013 following a Kickstarter campaign. Its mission is to enable independent journalists, writers, and content creators to earn a living online. It claims over three million installations or sites to date.

Substack and Ghost are both platforms that can be used for creating and publishing newsletters. However, they differ in terms of their type of platform, level of customization, cost, and business model. Ultimately, the best choice for you will depend on your specific needs and preferences.

**Newsletter Sales Funnels:**

A sales funnel represents the ideal path that companies hope buyers take to become customers. Most companies use the funnel concept as a method to track prospects as they move through sales stages and to align marketing and sales targets, activities, and processes. A newsletter sales funnel is a powerful tool that can be used for sales prospecting by guiding potential customers through the funnel stages.

**The first stage of the newsletter sales funnel is the awareness stage.** This is when a prospect finds your business online and registers for your email newsletters. The prospect may learn about a new brand through search engine results, social media or display ads. The goal of this stage is to capture the prospect's attention by providing valuable and relevant content that addresses their pain points and interests.

**The next stage of the newsletter sales funnel is the consideration stage.** This is where the prospect is actively evaluating your products or services and comparing them to other options in the market. The goal of this stage is to provide the prospect with detailed information about your products or services and demonstrate how they compare to other options.

**The fourth stage of the newsletter sales funnel is the conversion stage.** This is where the prospect becomes a customer by making a purchase. The goal of this stage is to provide the prospect with a clear and compelling call-to-action that makes it easy for them to make a purchase.

**The final stage of the newsletter sales funnel is the loyalty stage.** This is where the customer becomes a repeat customer by purchasing from your business again. The goal of this stage is to build loyalty and trust by providing excellent customer service and continuing to provide valuable and relevant content.

A newsletter sales funnel can be used for sales prospecting by guiding potential customers through the funnel stages, providing valuable and relevant content, building relationships, and making it easy for prospects to make a purchase. By using a newsletter sales funnel, businesses can increase their chances of converting prospects into customers and retaining them as repeat customers.

 **FROM THE FIELD**

When I send out newsletters, I use the traditional ad space along the top or sides to promote other ways to get prospects. For instance, I might create a banner to apply to be on my podcast, or one that offers a free marketing consultation with me.

 **AI TIP**

If you go to OpenAI, https://openai.com/, and sign up for a free Chat GPT account, you can use AI to help you write the perfect industry newsletter using keywords for your industry. Once your account is created, go to the prompt and type in: **Write a newsletter article about (industry topic)**

"SUCCESS IS A LITTLE LIKE WRESTLING
A GORILLA. YOU DON'T QUIT WHEN YOU
ARE TIRED –
YOU QUIT WHEN THE GORILLA IS TIRED."

-ROBERT STRAUSS

# BE A GUEST WRITER ON AN INDUSTRY BLOG

Guest blogging on an industry website can provide numerous benefits for your business and can be a valuable tool for sales prospecting. Not only does guest blogging allow you to showcase your expertise and reach a new audience, it can also help to establish credibility and build relationships with potential customers. By contributing high-quality content to an established industry website, you can increase visibility for your business and potentially generate leads. In this blog post, we'll explore the various ways that guest blogging can help with your sales prospecting efforts and provide tips on how to make the most of this opportunity.

**Establishing credibility and expertise:**

By consistently producing high-quality content on topics related to your industry, you can establish yourself as a knowledgeable and trusted source of information. This can help to attract potential customers who are interested in your products or services and are more likely to view you as a reliable source.

**Generating leads**:

A well-written and informative blog post can attract readers who are interested in the topic being discussed. By including a call-to-action (CTA) in your blog post, such as a form for readers to fill out to receive more information or a link to a product page, you can generate leads for your business.

**Engaging with potential customers:**

By including a comments section on your blog, you can engage with readers and respond to their questions or concerns. This can help to build a relationship with potential customers and can lead to increased interest in your products or services.

**Improving search engine optimization (SEO):**

By consistently producing high-quality content related to your industry, you can improve your website's ranking in search engine results. This can make it easier for potential customers to find your business and can lead to increased traffic to your website.

**Providing value to potential customers:**

By providing valuable and informative content on your industry blog, you can demonstrate your expertise and demonstrate the value that your business can provide to potential customers. This can help to increase interest in your products or services and can ultimately lead to increased sales.

Writing for an industry blog can help with sales prospecting by establishing credibility and expertise, generating leads, engaging with potential customers, improving SEO, and providing value to potential customers. By consistently producing high-quality content and actively engaging with readers, you can attract potential customers and increase interest in your business.

**Here is a sample email you could send to request to be a guest blogger:**

Dear [Blog Owner],

I hope this email finds you well. My name is [Your Name] and I am a [Your Job Title] with a background in [Your Expertise]. I am writing to express my interest in becoming a guest blogger for your website, [Website Name].

I am a huge fan of your blog and have been following it for some time. I believe that my unique perspective and expertise would add value to your audience and I would be honored to contribute to your blog.

I have attached a few examples of my writing for your review. My areas of expertise include [Expertise], and I am confident that I could provide engaging and informative content on these topics.

Thank you for considering my request. I look forward to the opportunity to contribute to your blog and engage with your readers.

Sincerely, [Your Name]

 **FROM THE FIELD**

This has more impact if you do a video email. If you go to OpenAI, https://openai.com/, and sign up for a free ChatGPT account, you can use AI to help you write the perfect guest blogger email using keywords for your industry. After you create the account, go to the prompt and type in: **Write an email requesting me to be a guest blogger for a website about _____**

 **AI TIP**

If you go to OpenAI, https://openai.com/, and sign up for a free Chat GPT account, you can use AI to help you write the perfect guest blog post or introduction email using keywords for your industry. Once your account is created, go to the prompt and type in: **Write a cold email asking for the opportunity to write a guest blog**

**Visit** www.ProspectingHacks.com **for free guides that will help you with your prospecting game plan.**

"SHOW ME YOUR FRIENDS, AND I'LL SHOW YOU YOUR FUTURE."

-DANNY HOLLAND

# GOOGLE ALERTS

You may have seen this being used in the Netflix movie "The Glass Onion". It's one of the clues that helped catch the killer!

Google Alerts is a free bot, or computer program, that automates various tasks, including prospecting, lead generation, marketing, and personal development tasks. It can be used to automate repetitive marketing, sales, and business tasks, making it an appealing tool for small businesses. Some considerations to keep in mind when using Google Alerts include the fact that it is a free product and that it is not always comprehensive. However, it can still be a valuable tool for prospecting.

**Here's a step-by-step guide on how to set up Google Alerts:**

Go to Google Alerts https://www.google.com/alerts

- In the box at the top, enter the topic you want to receive alerts for. You can enter any keyword or phrase, such as a product name, a person's name, or a news event.
- From the "Type" dropdown menu, select the type of content you want to receive alerts for. Options include "Everything," "News," "Blogs," "Web," "Video," "Books," and "Discussions."
- From the "How often" dropdown menu, select how often you want to receive alerts. Options include "As-it-happens," "At most once a day," and "At most once a week."
- From the "Source type" dropdown menu, select the type of sources you want to receive alerts from. Options include "Automatic," "News," "Blogs," "Web," "Video," "Books," and "Discussions."

- From the "Language" dropdown menu, select the language of the content you want to receive alerts for.
- In the "Deliver to" field, enter the email address you want to receive alerts at. You can also choose to receive alerts as a notification in the Google app on your phone.
- Click the "Create Alert" button.
- That's it! You should start receiving alerts for the topic you specified according to the frequency you selected. You can create multiple alerts for different topics by repeating these steps.

To edit or delete an alert, go to Google Alerts and click on the alert you want to modify. From there, you can change the settings or click the "Delete" button to remove the alert.

One way to generate leads is to use Google Alerts to monitor online conversations related to your business. When beginning the buying process, it is not uncommon for prospects to begin searching for information online. By setting up alerts for keywords related to your product or service, you can stay informed about potential sales prospects in your target market.

To do this, create alerts for questions that your prospects may ask, using terms that they are likely to use when searching for your product. For example, if you sell computer desks, you could create alerts for phrases like "best computer desk" or "best standing computer desk."

To cast a wider net, you can also include basic words like "who," "what," "when," "where," "why," "how much," "how," and "is," combined with your primary keywords and a wildcard operator (*). This will allow you to receive alerts for a variety of search terms related to your business. You can also set up alerts for your most frequently asked questions or those asked by your sales team. This can provide a steady stream of leads for your business.

One way to find potential customers or clients using Google Alerts is to follow authors, leaders, and industry colleagues. By tracking the people, you follow, you can gain valuable intelligence and insights that can help improve your products and services. This is also a great opportunity to network and connect with others in your industry. By following influential individuals and companies on social media, you can stay up to date on industry trends and developments and identify potential customers or partners. Additionally, by engaging with these individuals and sharing their content, you can increase your own visibility and establish yourself as a thought leader in your field.

Staying up to date with the activities of companies that you want to do business with is an important part of lead generation. By keeping track of these companies, you can ensure that you have current information when you need to make contact with them. This can also help you stay ahead of your competitors, especially if you are selling big-ticket items.

You can also find opportunities for new business by keeping track of your top customers. If you have a large customer list, focus on the top 1-5%, as they are likely responsible for the majority of your sales. By targeting these top customers, you may be able to spot opportunities for bigger and more frequent sales.

Using tools like Google Alerts can help you stay informed about the activities of your target companies and customers. Setting up targeted alerts can deliver timely information that can help you identify potential business opportunities and stay ahead of the competition.

Managing your company's reputation on social media is important for maintaining a positive image and attracting customers. One way to do this is to use Google Alerts to monitor all variations of your company name, as well as the names of your products and services and the names of your sales team or other individuals who come into contact with customers. This can help you stay informed about any mentions of your company and address both positive and negative feedback in a timely manner. If you receive a positive mention, you can reach out to the writer to thank them. If you receive a negative mention, you can try to resolve the issue by taking action to satisfy the disgruntled person. By using alerts to monitor your company's reputation, you can prevent small issues from becoming bigger ones and maintain a positive image on social media.

Tracking your competitors on social media can provide valuable insights and help you stay ahead of the competition. To do this, you can set up Google Alerts for your competitors' names, websites, and any other relevant keywords. For example, SEO blogger Matthew Woodward suggests using the following alerts:

**Site: [competitor's url]**

    **[competitor's name]**

    **"I think" [competitor's name]**
    **"Has anyone tried" [competitor's name]**
    **"This guest post by" [competitor's name]**

**Additional Google Alert Hacks:**

- Define your search queries to avoid alerts that have little to do with you or your company.
- Add quotations around your query to get only the best search results.
- Include common misspellings of your search term.
- Create multiple (but precise) alerts.
- Use a minus sign before a query to exclude results that include a specific word or phrase.
- Use an asterisk character known as a wildcard to match one or more words in a sentence.

Forums and blogs can be a valuable source for finding leads because they provide insight into what potential customers are looking for in terms of products or services. By using Google Alerts to monitor these platforms in real-time, you can quickly identify when and where leads are asking questions that your business can answer, allowing you to engage with pre-qualified leads.

**Use Google Alerts To Grow Your S.M.E. Status:**

By answering niche questions promptly, you can establish yourself as a Subject Matter Expert in your field and build trust with potential customers. To find fresh and relevant questions to answer using Google Alerts, you can:

- Monitor forums and blogs for industry-specific discussions and questions.
- Use Google Alerts to track keywords related to your business and receive real-time updates on relevant content.
- Join online communities or groups related to your industry to stay informed about current trends and questions.
- Regularly check frequently asked question (FAQ) pages on your website or on competitor's website to find common questions about your product or service.

By monitoring these alerts, you can see how your competitors are gaining publicity and use their tactics to your advantage. For example, if you see that a competitor is mentioned in several publications or blogs, you can add those publications to your press release list and craft similarly appealing press releases for your own business. Additionally, by staying up to date on your competitors' activities, you can identify opportunities to differentiate your business and stand out in the market.

 **FROM THE FIELD**

In addition to finding sales prospects, Google Alerts can also be used to monitor your backlink profile and measure the results of your link-building efforts, it can also help you identify allies or industry sites that you could partner with (such as through guest blogging).

"LUCK IS A WORD PEOPLE WHO ARE
LAZY USE TO DESCRIBE PEOPLE
WHO ARE HUSTLING."

-JON ACUFF

# GOOGLE BUSINESS PROFILE

If you're not utilizing Google Business Profile, https://www.google.com/business/, you could be missing out on an opportunity to attract more clients. Google Business Profile is a free platform that allows businesses to create a profile listing, making it easier for potential clients to find them online. Google is the most widely visited website in the world, with a 92% share of the search engine market. A Google Business Profile (formerly known as Google My Business) is a crucial tool for attracting new customers to your business through Google search and Maps. By creating a profile on this platform, you can increase the visibility of your business and make it easier for potential customers to find you online.

Having an optimized Google Business Profile allows you to showcase your business, including your location, services, and products. By creating a Google Business Profile, you can increase your visibility on Google services, such as Google Search, Google Maps, and Google Shopping. This platform is only available to businesses that have a physical location or meet with clients in other locations, like consultants or plumbers. By creating a Google Business Profile, you can provide potential customers with important information about your business and make it easier for them to find you online.

**Manage Your Online Business Profile:**

Your Google Business Profile (formerly known as Google My Business) gives you the ability to manage and update your contact information, business hours, and other important details as needed. You can use this platform to share updates about your business, such as changes to your services or temporary closures. This feature is especially useful during emergencies, like the COVID-19 pandemic. Google Business

Profiles have strong local SEO, so the information you share on your profile is more likely to rank higher than information on third-party sites that may not be up to date. By regularly updating your Google Business Profile, you can ensure that potential customers have accurate and current information about your business.

**Reviews, Both Good and Bad, Help Build Public Trust:**

Reviews can help build trust and credibility for your business. Google's combined star rating and space for detailed reviews allow customers to share their experience with your business on a public platform. This information can help future potential customers decide which businesses to visit and products to buy. While it can be intimidating to receive reviews on a public platform, it's important to remember that a combination of positive and negative reviews is often seen as more trustworthy than an overwhelmingly positive review history. You cannot choose which Google My Business reviews to display, but you can respond to all reviews to address any issues or concerns. By encouraging your customers to leave reviews and responding to them appropriately, you can build trust and credibility for your business through the Google Business Profile platform.

**How To Set Up:**

- Log into the Google Business Profile manager - https://www.google.com/business/
- Enter your business name.
- Enter your location.
- Fill in your contact information.
- Verify your business by requesting a postcard from Google to confirm your physical location.
- Customize your profile with a business description, hours of operation, messaging preferences, and photos.

After setting up your Google Business Profile and verifying it, the next step is to optimize it for better performance. Google ranks local businesses based on factors such as distance to the searcher, relevance, and prominence (determined by SEO, review score, number of reviews, and links).

**Complete all elements of your profile:**

A complete business profile appears more professional and reputable, which will help increase the number of people visiting and buying from you. Make sure to include information about the products or services you offer, your address, and your opening hours. Keep your profile up to date by making any necessary updates, such as changes to your opening hours.

**Verify your location:**

Verification adds credibility and trust to your profile, as well as improving your distance score and increasing the likelihood that your business shows up in local search results. Go to https://business.google.com to verify your location.

**Add real images and videos of your business:**

Business profiles with images get more clicks and requests for directions, so it's important to include high-quality images of your store or restaurant interiors, meals, menus, team members, and location. Use the same images for your logo and cover photo as on your social media profiles to boost brand recognition. To add photos or videos to your profile, go to the Photos or Video tab on the left-hand menu in your dashboard and follow the prompts.

**Include keywords in your profile:**

SEO keywords allow customers to find you and boost your relevance score. Use tools like Google Keyword Planner, https://ads.google.com/home/tools/keyword-planner/ to identify relevant keywords and insert them into your description in a natural way.

**Encourage and answer Google Business Profile reviews and questions:**

Reviews are crucial to the success of any business because they improve your Google ranking and attract more customers. Encourage customers to leave reviews by sending them a review request link from the "Share

Review" form on the bottom of your dashboard. Respond to all reviews, both positive and negative, to demonstrate your commitment to customer satisfaction. If you come across an inappropriate review, you can flag it for removal.

**Keep business information up to date**:

Make sure to immediately update your business information, such as hours, contact details, and other details, in the dashboard of your Google Business Profile. You can also create posts about news, promotions, events, or other updates. To create and publish posts, go to the Posts tab on the left-hand menu of the dashboard and follow the prompts.

**Add special features and attributes:**

Depending on your type of business, you may be able to add special features to your Google Business Profile. For example, restaurants and bars can display photos of dishes and menus, while hotels can display check-in and check-out times, amenities, highlights, class ratings, and sustainability practices. Service-oriented businesses may be able to add services, while healthcare providers in the US can display health insurance information. In addition to special features, you can also add attributes like free Wi-Fi, wheelchair accessibility, or outdoor seating in restaurants. To add attributes, go to the "Info" tab on the dashboard and select "Add Attributes" under "From the Business." Then, choose the appropriate attributes and click "Apply."

**Add your products (if applicable):**

Keeping an updated inventory of your products in your business profile can help customers determine if you offer what they're looking for and increase your chances of appearing in Google Shopping. To add products, go to the "Products" option on the left-hand menu of the dashboard and click "Get Started." Retail businesses in the US, Canada, Australia, the UK, or Ireland that have manufacturer barcodes on their products can use the "Pointy" tool to automatically upload their products to their profile.

Having a Google Business Profile is essential for businesses with a physical location, as it helps customers find your business on Google Search and Google Maps, read reviews, view photos, and make informed decisions about whether to visit and purchase from you. To get the most out of your Google Business Profile, be sure to optimize it and keep all information up to date. This will help provide a great experience for customers and potentially increase your business's growth.

 **AI TIP**

If you go to OpenAI, https://openai.com/, and sign up for a free Chat GPT account, you can use AI to help you write the perfect Google Business Profile using keywords for your industry. Once your account is created, go to the prompt and type in: **Write a Google business profile with SEO keywords for (your product or service)**

You can also use Chat GPT to search for relevant keywords for your industry. Another clever SEO tip here is when you respond to reviews on your Google profile, ask Chat GPT to write your review responses using your keywords!

"COASTING ONLY TAKES YOU DOWNHILL."

-ROGER CRAWFORD

# SOCIAL MEDIA

Social media networking is a powerful tool that you should consider adding to your toolkit. According to research from HubSpot, while 90% of executives won't respond to cold calls, 75% of them use social media to make buying decisions. This means that it is crucial for sales professionals to have a presence on social media platforms where their target audience is active.

**SOCIAL MEDIA SALES FUNNEL**

**AWARENESS**

Use social media platforms such as Facebook, YouTube, blogs, and Google to engage your target audience with relevant content and attract potential leads.

**INTEREST**

Offer a free resource, such as a PDF, e-book, gift, or video tutorial, to individuals who are interested in learning about your products and services. In exchange for this resource, ask for their email address as a way to continue the conversation and provide value to them.

**DESIRE**

By providing you with their email, the target audience has demonstrated interest in your brand. Now is an opportunity to offer additional value and build trust with your lead.

**ACTION**

This is an opportune moment to finalize the transaction and have the target audience purchase your product or services. By now, the initial "cold" lead should have become familiar with and developed trust in your brand, making them more likely to take action and make a purchase.

AWARENESS

INTEREST

DESIRE

ACTION

**But how can you effectively use social media networking to increase your sales?**

**Find your audience:**

Social media networking is a lot like traditional networking. You aren't going to find quality prospects by showing up anywhere and everywhere. Before you focus on one or two social platforms, determine where your target audience is active. Search for relevant conversations - about your products, industry, or customers' common interests - on social media platforms. LinkedIn tends to have a stronger pull for B2B industries, but that doesn't mean that leaders at corporations aren't on Twitter and Instagram. Good content attracts people, and if you follow industry experts, you will likely find like-minded people who will respond to your social networking follow, too.

**Listen more than you share (at least at first):**

Once you've identified the bigger social sites for your audience, listen and use what you hear - recurring concerns, needs, and questions - as leverage for real conversations. Listen for a while, then ease into networking by commenting on blogs and websites and joining live chats. Get involved in relevant conversations where you can offer helpful answers and advice, not product or service solutions.

**Create a fitting persona:**

Yes, you want to be yourself when you build a social media networking presence. Most importantly, you want to be your **best** self. Build accounts on platforms your customers and prospects use. Join communities where you have something valuable to contribute (that's not a pitch). Get to know the norms and expectations for the communities before you share. To find the right groups on LinkedIn, search for topics that are your expertise, not just your industry. To build a trustworthy persona, share information from reputable sources before you spout off your advice. Answer direct questions and ask for permission to give unsolicited advice in your communities to build deeper credibility.

**Follow the right users:**

The adage "You're only as good as the company you keep" is true for social media, too. Use a tool such as Followerwonk, https://followerwonk.com/ or Tweeple, https://tweeplesearch.com, to search Twitter profiles or keywords to get a list of top-rated users in your or your customers' industry. Hashtagify can do similar things for Instagram.

**Follow the right people and companies:**

Dream big. Pull together a list of everything from the mom-and-pops to mega-brands that you'd like as clients and find them on Twitter, Facebook, and LinkedIn (those three are still the most used in business). Then stay up to date on what they're doing. At the very least, you can say congrats when they announce good things. Like, retweet, and otherwise engage with them as much as possible to create your presence. Even better: Offer demos when they mention a need you can fulfill.

**Yes, follow your competition:**

Another important adage for social media networking is "Keep your friends close and your enemies closer." Follow your competitors to stay up to date on industry developments and opportunities for collaboration or demo offers.

**Personal branding is key:**

Your social media profiles are a reflection of you and your brand. Make sure your profiles are complete and professional. Consistent posting also helps to increase your visibility and credibility on social media.

**Connect with your audience through personalized outreach:**

Once you've established a presence on social media and have identified your target audience, it's time to start building relationships. This can be done through personalized outreach, such as direct messages or email. Make an effort to get to know your audience and understand their needs and pain points. By building relationships and showing that you genuinely care about helping them, you increase the chances of making a sale.

**Use the search function provided by the social media platform.**

**Run searches for:**

- Your own hashtags, your competitor's hashtags, and industry-related hashtags
- Your business name and your competitors' business names
- Your city or region and product category (e.g. "mechanic Orlando")
- Your product or service category and "recommendation" (e.g. "web designer recommendation")

**Once you've found potential customers, engage with them by:**

- Answering questions they have asked
- Suggesting related products
- Simply following them

**Remember to be respectful and helpful in your interactions with potential customers to establish trust and credibility.**

**Ask Your Current Customers:**

- One effective way to identify potential customers on social media is to ask your current customers which platforms they use.

**For brick-and-mortar businesses, you can include a line on contest entry forms or feedback forms for customers to write links to their social media profiles.**

**For online businesses, you can include a field on your contact form and email opt-in form for customers to provide their social media profile links.**

**You can also ask your email subscribers where you can find them online, including their website or blog URLs and their social media profiles.**

By collecting this information from your current customers, you can identify potential customers and engage with them on the social media platforms they use. This can help to build relationships and increase the chances of making a sale.

Social media networking is a powerful tool for sales professionals looking to make connections and increase their sales. By finding your audience, listening more than you share, creating a fitting persona, following the right users and companies, personal branding, and connecting with your audience through personalized outreach, you can effectively use social media to build relationships and increase your chances of making a sale.

If you go to OpenAI, https://openai.com/, and sign up for a free Chat GPT account, you can use AI to help you write the perfect social media posts, with hashtags, using keywords for your industry. Once your account is created, go to the prompt and type in: **Write a Facebook post about (your product or industry)** Or, maybe: **Write ten Tweets with hashtags about (your product or industry)**

"EVERYONE HAS TO GET GOOD AT ONE
OF TWO THINGS: PLANTING IN THE
SPRING OR BEGGING IN THE FALL."

-JIM ROHN

# COLLABORATE WITH SOCIAL MEDIA AND BUSINESS INFLUENCERS

Influencer marketing is a strategy that involves partnering with individuals who have a large social media following and the ability to influence their audience. These influencers can help promote a brand's product or service through paid advertisements, free giveaways, or endorsements. This type of marketing can generate significant brand awareness and loyalty and reach a larger audience at a lower cost than traditional advertising methods.

Influencer marketing is a valuable strategy for both B2C and B2B brands, with 86% of B2B brands finding it effective. Agencies can also benefit from influencer marketing by using their clients as referral sources and creating case studies to share on their website, social media, and ads.

To create an influencer marketing strategy, it's important to identify the goals of the campaign and the target audience, research and select appropriate influencers, and create a clear plan for content creation and promotion. It's also important to track and measure the results of the campaign to optimize future efforts.

Some tips for successful influencer marketing include building genuine relationships with influencers, providing them with clear guidelines and expectations, and offering unique and valuable experiences or products. By implementing a well-planned influencer marketing strategy, businesses can increase their brand awareness, generate leads, and drive sales.

Influencer marketing can be an effective way to increase prospecting for your business by using celebrities, athletes, bloggers, and other influential figures to promote your brand and reach a larger audience. To create a successful influencer marketing strategy, it's important to choose influencers who align with your brand's values and goals, and to pay them fairly. You should also have a clear plan in place for what you would like to achieve with your influencer collaboration, including whether you will provide content and supporting information or if the influencer will be responsible for creating their own.

Another way to use influencer marketing for prospecting is by partnering with influencers for events or webinars. This can allow you to reach a larger audience and establish yourself as a thought leader in your industry. You can also consider offering influencers incentives or commissions for any sales they generate through their partnership with your business.

Influencer marketing can be a powerful tool for increasing prospecting for your business. By choosing the right influencers and creating a clear plan for your collaboration, you can reach a larger audience, establish yourself as a thought leader, and drive growth and success for your business.

**Here is a sample email you could use to reach out to an influencer:**

Dear [Influencer's Name],

I hope this email finds you well. My name is [Your Name] and I am the [Your Job Title] at [Your Company]. I am writing to express my interest in collaborating with you on a social media campaign.

I am a huge fan of your content and believe that your influence and reach would be a valuable asset to our marketing efforts. We are currently looking for influencers to promote our [Product/Service] and believe that you would be the perfect fit for our brand.

To start, I would love to learn more about your interests and any current collaborations you are working on. We are open to exploring a variety of partnership opportunities, including sponsored posts, giveaways, and product reviews.

Thank you for considering my request. I look forward to the opportunity to work with you and help promote your content to our audience.

Sincerely, [Your Name]

## FROM THE FIELD

This has more impact if you do a video email.

## AI TIP

If you go to OpenAI, https://openai.com/, and sign up for a free ChatGPT account, you can use AI to help you write the perfect influencer email using keywords for your industry. After you create the account, go to the prompt and type in "write an email to a social media influencer about partnership opportunities."

**Using a social media influencer agency:**

Social media influencer agencies help businesses connect with popular social media personalities and influencers to promote their products or services. If you are looking to work with an influencer agency, it is important to do your research and choose a reputable and reliable agency. Here is a list of some of the top social media influencer agencies:

**Pulse Advertising**: https://www.pulse-advertising.com/

Pulse Advertising is a global influencer marketing agency with a wide network of influencers on various social media platforms. The agency has worked with top clients such as HM, LVMH, Marriott, and Unilever, and is a listed Google Partner, Instagram Partner, and Facebook Marketing Partner.

**The Influencer Marketing Factory:**
https://theinfluencermarketingfactory.com/

The Influencer Marketing Factory is one of the top national and global influencer marketing agencies. The agency has had successful campaigns with companies such as Google, Amazon, Snapchat, and Sony Music. They focus on matching the right influencer to the right brand.

**Upfluence Inc:** https://www.upfluence.com/

Upfluence is known for its influencer marketing platform, but also acts as an influencer agency. The agency provides clients with full software access to track the progress of their campaigns, which are managed by a dedicated team of influence experts.

Other reputable social media influencer agencies include Social Native, Fohr, Linqia, Collective Bias, and The Shelf. It is important to do your research and choose an agency that has a track record of success and can provide the services that meet your needs.

**Automated Influencer Outreach:**

**NinjaOutreach:** https://ninjaoutreach.com/

Create effective influencer marketing campaigns by filtering through millions of influencers' insights to find the one that captures your target audiences attention.

"DON'T LET YESTERDAY USE UP
TOO MUCH OF TODAY."

-KAREN LAMB

# INSTAGRAM PROSPECTING

Instagram can be a valuable tool for businesses to connect with prospects and effectively engage with them. In fact, Instagram has enormous potential for lead generation and businesses with strong social media marketing strategies are taking advantage of it.

- 400 million active users
- Over 60% log in daily

Engagement on Instagram is 10 times higher than Facebook, 54 times higher than Pinterest, and 84 times higher than Twitter (at least, what's left of Twitter).

And the best part is, 80% of Facebook survey respondents say they use Instagram to decide whether or not to make a purchase. If you're not already using Instagram for lead generation, you're missing out on some incredible opportunities to grow your marketing network.

**Creating an Instagram account is easy and only takes a few minutes.**

**Here's a step-by-step guide on how to do it:**

- Download the Instagram app on your mobile device. You can find it in the App Store (for iPhone/iPad), Play Store (for Android), or Windows Phone Store (for Windows phone).
- Open the Instagram app once it's downloaded to your device.
- Click the option to register. You have two options: through your Facebook account or with your email address.
- If you choose to register with your email address, you'll need to enter your full name, email address, and a password. If you

choose to register with your Facebook account, you'll need to log in to your Facebook account and grant Instagram access to your information.

- Once you've completed the registration process, you'll be taken to your Instagram feed. From here, you can start following other users, liking and commenting on their posts, and uploading your own photos and videos.

But how do you actually generate leads on Instagram? It's not just about hashtags and the occasional post. You need a solid strategy to turn Instagram followers into customers.

**Targeting:**

Clearly define the image of the kind of leads you want to generate on Instagram. This will help you determine the steps you need to take in the lead generation process. Ask yourself questions like, "How do my prospects spend their free time?", "What goals and values do they have?", and "What kind of media interests do they have?"

**Optimization:**

Set up your Instagram account in a way that maximizes lead generation. Use your brand name as your account name, add a recognizable and professional profile picture, choose a relevant category, and include a link to your website in the bio.

**Hashtags:**

Hashtags are a powerful tool for reaching a larger audience on social media platforms like Instagram. By using relevant hashtags in your posts, you can increase the visibility of your content and reach a wider audience of potential customers.

So, how do hashtags work? Hashtags work by allowing people to search for content using keywords or phrases. When you use a hashtag in a social media post, that post will be added to a feed of all the other posts that have used the same hashtag. This means that if someone searches for that hashtag, they will see your post along with all the other posts that have used the same hashtag.

To use hashtags effectively for sales prospecting, it is important to choose hashtags that are relevant to your business and the products or services you offer.

For example, if you sell eco-friendly products, you might use hashtags like #sustainability or #greenliving. By using these hashtags, you can reach people who are interested in sustainability and are more likely to be interested in your products.

**Hashtags can be used in any word or phrase, but there are a few main types to consider:**

- Descriptive hashtags
- Branded hashtags
- Trending hashtags

Descriptive hashtags describe the content of your post, branded hashtags promote your brand, and trending hashtags are popular hashtags that are being widely used at the moment.

In addition to using relevant hashtags, it is also important to **use them sparingly**. Using too many hashtags can make your post look spammy and can turn off potential customers. Aim for one to three relevant hashtags per post to maximize their effectiveness.

Hashtags are a valuable tool for reaching a larger audience and increasing the visibility of your business on social media. By using relevant hashtags and using them sparingly, you can effectively use hashtags for sales prospecting and reach more potential customers.

**How you can drive more traffic to your Instagram account:**

**Collaborate with influencers:**

Partnering with influencers can help you reach a larger, targeted audience and increase the credibility of your brand. Just make sure to choose influencers who align with your values and target audience.

**Engage with your followers:**

Respond to comments and messages, and show your personality. This will help you build a community of loyal followers and increase the chances of turning them into customers.

**Add Action Buttons to your profile:**

If you have a business account on Instagram, you can add action buttons to your profile, such as a link to your email, phone number, and business address, as well as "Book," "Reserve," and "Get Tickets" buttons that lead to forms from Instagram providers like Appointy, Eventbrite, OpenTable, Resy, and others.

**Optimize the link in your bio:**

Use the limited link space in your bio to its full potential by directing customers to your desired objective, whether it be a newsletter subscription, product sales, or a survey. Make sure to keep the link short and include UTM parameters to make it trackable.

**Design a landing page that delivers:**

Once someone clicks on your link, you need a landing page that won't make them regret their decision. Make sure the page is scannable, visually appealing, and has content that matches what people are expecting to find.

**Use the "Swipe Up" feature on Instagram Stories:**

If your account has over 10,000 followers, you can use the "Swipe Up" feature on Instagram Stories to add links. This is a great way to drive traffic to your website or landing page, as one-third of the most viewed Instagram Stories are from businesses and brand-led stories have a completion rate of 85%.

**Tailor creative around your goal:**

Use a strong call-to-action, such as "swipe up," "shop now," or "click the link in our bio," and pair it with the right content to fulfill your goal. Make sure your visuals and call-to-action work together and leave room for the call-to-action in your creative.

**Use the "LIVE" logo:**

Adding the "LIVE" logo over your Instagram profile will make it more prominent and visible to your followers. Being live on Instagram makes your brand more relatable as there's a human feel to it.

**Be consistent:**

Consistency is key when it comes to building engagement on Instagram. Make sure to post regularly and at optimal times to reach your target audience.

**Use Instagram messaging tools:**

Using Instagram messaging tools like MobileMonkey's DM tools can help you turn Instagram traffic into website traffic. These tools allow you to instantly reply to DMs and auto-respond to comments on your posts.

**Use Instagram Stories and IGTV:**

Instagram Stories and IGTV are great ways to create more engaging content that can help drive traffic to your website. Use them to share behind-the-scenes footage, tutorials, or product demos.

**Use Instagram's shopping feature:**

Instagram's shopping feature allows you to tag products in your posts and stories, making it easy for customers to purchase your products directly from Instagram.

**Analyze your analytics:**

Keep track of your Instagram analytics to see which posts are performing the best and which are driving the most traffic to your website. Use this information to adjust your strategy and improve your results over time.

**Run an Instagram contest:**

An Instagram contest can be a great way for businesses to engage with their audience, increase their brand visibility, and potentially drive sales. Just make sure to follow Instagram's contest guidelines and offer a prize that aligns with your brand.

**Here are some steps to set up and launch an Instagram contest for your business:**

**Determine your goals and objectives:**

Before you begin planning your contest, it's important to know what you want to achieve. Are you looking to increase your brand's visibility? Generate leads? Boost sales? Knowing your goals will help you create a contest that is tailored to your needs.

**Choose a prize:**

The prize you offer should be relevant to your target audience and aligned with your business goals. It could be a product or service you offer, or something more general that would appeal to your audience.

**Determine your entry requirements:**

A popular method of entry is to have people like your photo announcing the contest, leave a comment, and follow your account. You could also require participants to post a photo or video with a specific hashtag and theme, or to tag your brand in their post. Ask participants to follow you or create a post in order to enter. Ask participants to like, follow, share, or tag your brand in order to enter.

### Choose a hashtag:

A hashtag is a way for people to easily search for and find your contest. Choose a hashtag that is relevant to your business and contest, and make sure to include it in all of your contest-related posts and promotions.

### Create contest rules and guidelines:

It's important to set clear rules and guidelines for your contest to ensure a fair and enjoyable experience for all participants. This should include details such as the start and end date of the contest, how winners will be selected, and any eligibility requirements.

### Promote your contest:

Once you have all the details of your contest in place, it's time to start promoting it to your audience. This could include posts on your Instagram account, as well as promoting the contest on other social media platforms, through email marketing, or on your website.

### Monitor and engage with participants:

As your contest is underway, be sure to monitor and engage with participants. This could include responding to comments, answering questions, and thanking people for participating.

### Choose and announce the winners:

When the contest is over, choose the winners using the method you specified in your contest rules. Announce the winners on your Instagram account, and consider reaching out to them privately to get their contact information for prize fulfillment.

Launching an Instagram contest can provide a number of benefits for sales prospecting. By engaging with your audience and increasing your brand visibility, you can generate leads and potentially drive sales. An Instagram contest can also help you build relationships with your audience, which can lead to repeat business and customer loyalty.

By following these tips, you can increase traffic to your Instagram account and drive more visitors to your website. Remember to be consistent, engage with your audience, and use Instagram's features to your advantage.

 AI TIP

If you go to OpenAI, https://openai.com/, and sign up for a free Chat GPT account, you can use AI to help you find keywords and hashtags you can you use in your posts for your industry. Once your account is created, go to the prompt and type in: **Write 20 keywords for (your industry)** Second prompt: **Write hashtags for each keyword**

"THERE ARE NO TRAFFIC JAMS
ALONG THE EXTRA MILE."

-ROGER STAUBACH

# FACEBOOK PROSPECTING

Facebook is a powerful platform for driving traffic to your website and increasing brand awareness for your business. **Here are some detailed tips for getting more traffic to your Facebook Business Page:**

**Set up a Facebook Business Page:**

The first step in using Facebook for sales prospecting is to set up a Facebook Business Page. This will allow you to create a professional presence on the platform and provide information about your products or services to potential customers. https://www.facebook.com/business/tools/facebook-pages/get-started

**Engage with potential customers on your Facebook Page:**

Once you have set up a Facebook Business Page and are using it to post valuable content, make sure to engage with potential customers who comment on your posts or send you messages. Responding to comments and messages in a timely and professional manner can help to build relationships with potential customers and establish trust.

**Use your personal profile to connect with potential customers:**

In addition to using your business page, you can also use your personal profile to connect with potential customers. Participate in relevant groups and post valuable content that showcases your expertise. This can help to establish you as a thought leader in your industry and can encourage potential customers to send you friend requests or messages.

**Utilize Facebook Pages to connect with potential customers:**

As an administrator of a Facebook Page, you can switch your identity to the business and join the conversation on competitors' pages to prospect for fans of your own.

**Use Facebook Live to connect with potential customers:**

Facebook Live is a feature that allows you to stream live video to your followers. You can use this feature to host webinars or Q&A sessions, or to give potential customers a behind-the-scenes look at your business. This can be an effective way to engage with potential customers and build relationships.

**Utilize Facebook Messenger to connect with potential customers:**

Facebook Messenger is a messaging platform that allows you to communicate with potential customers in real-time. You can use this feature to answer questions or provide information about your products or services.

**Use Facebook Groups to connect with potential customers:**

Facebook Groups are online communities where people with similar interests can connect and discuss topics. You can use this feature to participate in relevant groups and connect with potential customers.

**Use Facebook analytics:**

Use Facebook's Analysis tab to get data on the best post type, length, and time to post for your topic. This will help you create updates that send more traffic back to your site.

**Pick the best ad objective:**

When creating a campaign, it's important to choose the right ad objective. There are three different objectives for Facebook ads: Awareness, Consideration and Conversion. Pick the one that is most suitable for your business.

**Offer exclusive deals:**

Offering exclusive deals can incentivize page visits and followers. Make sure you mention that the deal is exclusive to your Facebook followers to encourage them to visit your page.

**Run contests:**

Running contests, especially voting contests, can help drive traffic and engagement with your page.

**Create a Facebook Popup:**

Creating a Facebook Popup will help you to increase engagement and followers.

**Collaborate with influencers:**

Collaborating with influencers in your niche can help you reach a wider audience and drive more traffic to your Facebook Business Page.

**Use Facebook's Call-to-Action button:**

Use Facebook's Call-to-Action button to direct users to your website or landing page.

**Analyze your analytics:**

Keep track of your Facebook analytics to see which posts are performing the best and which are driving the most traffic to your website. Use this information to adjust your strategy and improve your results over time.

**Utilize Instagram to showcase your products or services:**

Instagram is a visual social media platform that is owned by Facebook. You can use Instagram to showcase your products or services and engage with potential customers.

## Utilize WhatsApp to connect with potential customers:

WhatsApp is a messaging platform that is owned by Facebook. You can use WhatsApp to connect with potential customers and provide them with information about your products or services.

By utilizing these tools and features, you can effectively use Facebook for sales prospecting. Don't be afraid to experiment with different strategies to see what works best for your business. Remember to always be professional and provide value to your potential customers, as this can help to establish trust and build relationships that can lead to increased sales.

If you go to OpenAI, https://openai.com/, and sign up for a free Chat GPT account, you can use AI to help you write the perfect Facebook posts, with hashtags, using keywords for your industry. Once your account is created, go to the prompt and type in: **Write a Facebook post about (your product or industry)**

**Visit** www.ProspectingHacks.com **for free guides that will help you with your prospecting game plan.**

"A GOAL WITHOUT ACTIVITY IS A DREAM."

-ROBERT KYSLINGER

# LINKEDIN PROSPECTING

LinkedIn, www.linkedin.com, and is an online professional social media platform. Currently it has (as of the writing of this book) 875 million professional members in more than 200 countries and territories worldwide.

LinkedIn's mission is to connect the world's professionals to make them more productive and successful. There are many ways to leverage this platform for professional gain (and many more books, blogs, and YouTube channels). I won't get into the weeds too much, but, I do want to share some of my favorite hacks you can utilize on LinkedIn for your sales prospecting efforts.

- LinkedIn's "Groups" feature can be a good way to find new prospects by joining and participating in groups related to your industry or target market. By engaging with group members and contributing valuable content, you can build your reputation and potentially find new prospects through your participation in the group.
- Browsing users who have interacted with your own posts on LinkedIn can also be a way to find new prospects. Under the "Posts & Activity" section of your profile, you can see a feed of all the articles and posts you have shared, along with everyone who has interacted with each one. By clicking the "Your followers" tab on the left sidebar, you can see who has recently followed you and may be a good new prospect.
- See who has commented on your existing prospects' posts. By paying attention to the comments on your connections' posts, you may find potential good fits for your product who are active on LinkedIn. In addition, you can use their comments as

a starting point for an InMail message, such as praising their insight and offering a related perspective, sharing a relevant article, or asking if they have considered a specific fact or data point.

- Look for individuals who have recently changed jobs. When someone takes on a new role, they may be more open to considering new products or services, so reaching out to them at this time can be a good opportunity to land a new customer. To find out which of your connections have recently joined a new company, you can check the "Notifications" tab and look for updates on job changes, birthdays, or new blog posts.

- The "People Also Viewed" sidebar on LinkedIn is a useful tool for finding potential new customers or prospects who are similar to your existing contacts. To use this feature, simply visit the profile of one of your best customers or prospects and look to the right for the "People Also Viewed" box. This will show you other users who are similar to your contact, allowing you to potentially turn one prospect into several.

- Investigate the networks of your competitors. Often, it can be easier to sell to a competitor's customer than to try to find a completely new prospect with no experience with your product. You can search other LinkedIn members' networks (provided they are not protected) to find connections of rival salespeople, who are likely connected with their prospects and customers.

- Scrolling through skill endorsements on LinkedIn can also be a useful way to find new prospects. By looking at the "Skills" section of a customer or prospect's profile and checking out who has endorsed them, you may find that people who are similar to your target customer have also endorsed them.

- The LinkedIn alumni search tool is another useful way to find new prospects. By copying https://www.linkedin.com/edu/alumni into your browser, you can get a list of prospects who attended the same school as you, which can provide a natural connection for reaching out to them.

**Find Prospects Using Boolean Search Criteria:**

A fun way to find new prospects is to play with Boolean search operators in Google to find specific profiles. These operators include quotation marks, OR, AND, and NOT, and can help you narrow down your search results.

**Quotation marks: Find results with the exact phrase.**

**OR: Find results that contain either search term A or search term B.**

**AND: Find results that contain both search term A and search term B.**

**NOT: Find results that contain search term A but not search term B.**

**Make sure to add "site:linkedin.com/in" to the beginning of your search query.**

**Here are three example Boolean searches for LinkedIn contacts:**

"software engineer" AND "San Francisco" This search will return LinkedIn profiles for software engineers who are located in San Francisco. The AND operator allows you to narrow your search by combining multiple keywords.

"project manager" NOT "consultant" This search will return LinkedIn profiles for project managers who are not consultants. The NOT operator allows you to exclude certain keywords from your search.

"product manager" OR "product marketing" This search will return LinkedIn profiles for product managers or product marketers. The OR operator allows you to broaden your search by including multiple keywords.

**You can find more information and tips on using boolean search on LinkedIn with the following link:**

https://www.linkedin.com/pulse/linkedin-boolean-search-advanced-tips-growth-houston-golden

 **AI TIP**

If you go to OpenAI, https://openai.com/, and sign up for a free Chat GPT account, you can use AI to help you write the perfect social media posts, with hashtags, using keywords for your industry. Once your account is created, go to the prompt and type in: **Write a LinkedIn post about (your product or industry)**

**Visit** www.ProspectingHacks.com **for free guides that will help you with your prospecting game plan.**

"IF YOU ONLY DO THE BARE MINIMUM,
DON'T EXPECT ANYTHING BUT
BARE MINIMUM RESULTS."

-J.J. WATT

 # TIKTOK PROSPECTING

TikTok has exploded in popularity over the past few years, and while it may have started out as a platform for singing and dancing, it has become much more than that. Businesses can use TikTok to build their brand, showcase their personality, generate leads and sign-ups, and increase their sales conversion rate. However, there are a few misconceptions about TikTok that are important to address. One is that it is only for a younger audience and only for dancing. While it may have started out that way, TikTok's target audience is now all-inclusive, with users ranging from age 13 to 113. Another misconception is that TikTok is only for smaller businesses or solopreneurs. While it is certainly a great platform for those groups, it can also be valuable for larger corporations.

The TikTok algorithm is extremely intelligent and can help target the ideal user, and early adopters of technology often flock to platforms like TikTok. If you're interested in using TikTok for your business, start small and see what kind of traction you get with around 30 test posts. The potential for massive growth is there, as long as you create high-quality and engaging content. Just be sure to familiarize yourself with TikTok's community guidelines and stay up to date on any changes to the platform.

TikTok allows you to connect with your audience on a deeper level and reach new markets. While there are plenty of social media platforms out there, TikTok reigns supreme in terms of going viral. Just about anyone can get millions of views on TikTok thanks to the clever algorithm. And as a brand, you have even more potential for reaching millions of people since you already have customers who care about you. Plus, you don't need millions of followers to reach a large audience on TikTok, unlike on Instagram, Facebook, and Twitter.

**Here is a step by step guide on how to create a TikTok account:**

- Download the TikTok app from the App Store or Google Play.
- Open the app and tap on the "Profile" icon located in the bottom right corner.
- Choose a method to sign up, either by email or phone number. Make sure to use a valid email address or phone number, as it will be needed for login and password recovery.
- Enter your date of birth and create a password.
- Choose a username for your TikTok account. It is recommended to choose a unique and memorable username that reflects your personal brand or content theme.
- Confirm your email address or phone number by following the verification steps provided in the app.
- Once you have completed the sign-up process, you can start creating and sharing TikTok videos by clicking on the "+" button located at the bottom of the app.
- *Note: You may be asked to grant TikTok access to your photos, camera, and microphone in order to create and share videos.

So how does the TikTok algorithm work? It uses various factors to determine your interests at any given moment, such as watching a video from beginning to end, using hashtags and sounds, getting likes, shares, and comments, and taking into account your location and language. This allows TikTok to quickly identify if you have an interest in a specific topic, hashtag, sound, or trend and start recommending similar content.

**To increase your chances of success with TikTok marketing, try these tips:**

**Use TikTok's in-platform tools:** Use TikTok's in-platform tools to add captions and text to your content. This can help the algorithm understand what topics you're covering and who your content will be most relevant to.

**Switch to a business account:** Regular users can switch to a business account in just four quick steps. This will give you access to business-specific features and analytics.

**Engage with comments:** If people are commenting on your videos, keep the conversation going. Respond to comments and messages and use them to build relationships with your followers.

**Use Hashtags:** Use relevant hashtags in your posts to make them more discoverable to users who are searching for content related to your niche.

**Create engaging content:** Create engaging and appropriate content for your target audience. Use humor, creativity, and storytelling to grab their attention.

**Collaborate with influencers:** Collaborating with influencers in your niche can help you reach a wider audience and drive more traffic to your TikTok account.

**Run Contests:** Running contests, especially voting contests, can help drive traffic and engagement with your page.

**Use TikTok's built-in e-commerce features:** TikTok has built-in e-commerce features that allow you to connect with customers, create shopping experiences, and drive sales.

**Analyze your analytics:** Keep track of your TikTok analytics to see which posts are performing the best and which are driving the most engagement. Use this information to adjust your strategy and improve your results over time.

With these strategies, you can take your TikTok marketing game to the next level and potentially reach millions of people. It's important not to get intimidated with all that is possible with TikTok, remember, your kids are already professionals at it. Having said that, the largest demographic on the platform at the time of this writing are users over 30, find your audience and grow your prospect pool!

## "YOUR CUSTOMER'S PERCEPTION IS YOUR REALITY."

-KATE ZABRISKIE

# START A YOUTUBE CHANNEL

Having a YouTube channel for your business can offer numerous benefits, including the potential to increase prospecting and sales possibilities.

**Creating a YouTube channel is a simple process that allows you to share your own videos and content with a wider audience. Here's a step-by-step guide on how to set up a YouTube channel:**

- Go to YouTube and sign in with your Google account. If you don't have a Google account, you'll need to create one first.
- Click on your profile picture in the top right corner and select "My channel" from the dropdown menu.
- Click on the "Create a new channel" button.
- Enter a name for your channel and upload a profile picture. You can also enter a description for your channel if you wish.
- Click on the "Create channel" button to finish creating your channel.
- Once your channel is set up, you can start uploading videos to it. Here's how to upload a video to your YouTube channel:
- Go to your channel page and click on the camera icon in the top right corner.
- Click on the "Select files" button to select the video file you want to upload from your computer.
- Enter a title and description for your video, and choose any relevant tags or categories.
- Click on the "Publish" button to upload your video to YouTube.

That's it! Your video will now be live on your YouTube channel for others to watch and share. You can upload as many videos as you like to your channel, and you can also customize the look and feel of your channel by going to the "Channel settings" page.

**YouTube Getting Started:** https://www.youtube.com/creators/how-things-work/getting-started/

**Here are just a few of the ways that having a YouTube channel can help drive growth and success for your business:**

**Increased visibility:**

With a YouTube channel, you can reach new audiences and become a go-to source for information in your industry. Imagine the look of shock on your competitors' faces when they see you showing up in the recommended videos of their target audience.

**Enhanced content marketing:**

By creating quality videos that provide value to your audience, you can establish yourself as an expert in your field and attract new leads and customers. Bonus points if you can make it entertaining, because who doesn't love a good laugh while learning something new?

**Improved customer engagement:**

By sharing videos that showcase your expertise and experiences, you can create a sense of community and belonging among your viewers. This can help strengthen your relationships with your audience and encourage them to continue watching your videos. Plus, it's always nice to make a connection with your customers beyond just trying to sell them something.

**Increased sales:**

Ultimately, having a YouTube channel can lead to increased sales for your business. By increasing your visibility, enhancing your content marketing efforts, and improving customer engagement, you can create a more favorable environment for generating new leads and closing sales. And who doesn't love a little extra cash in their pockets?

**Invite your clients (and potential clients) to be guests on your show!**

It's important to keep in mind that inviting your clients to be on your YouTube channel is just one aspect of a successful marketing strategy. To maximize the benefits of having your clients as guests, it's essential to have a clear plan in place for promoting their appearance and engaging with your audience. This can involve promoting the video on social media, email marketing, and other channels, as well as encouraging your clients to share the video with their own networks.

It's crucial to ensure that the video is high-quality and provides value to your viewers. This can involve having a well-planned and structured interview or presentation, as well as ensuring that the video has good lighting and sound quality. By putting in the effort to create a high-quality video, you can increase the chances of your clients' appearance on your YouTube channel being successful and driving business results.

Having your clients as guests on your YouTube channel can offer numerous benefits for your business, including increased exposure, improved credibility, enhanced content, improved customer loyalty, and increased sales. By carefully planning and promoting your clients' appearance on your YouTube channel, you can maximize these benefits and drive growth and success for your business.

**Different ways to grow your YouTube subscribers:**

**Use a compelling title:** Use a compelling title that tells viewers what they can expect from watching your video.

**Select a thumbnail:** Select a thumbnail that captures attention and conveys what people will see in the video.

**Add annotations:** Add informative, relevant, or entertaining annotations to engage viewers before, during, or after they watch your video.

**Target the right keywords:** YouTube is a search engine (it's the second largest web search engine, the first being Google), and targeting the right keywords can help you grow your subscriber count.

**Optimize your video for SEO:** Optimizing your video for SEO by including relevant keywords in your title, tags, and description, can help increase visibility and attract more viewers.

**Collaborate with other YouTubers:** Collaborating with other YouTubers in your niche can help members to be consistent, engage with your audience.

**Promote your channel:** Promote your channel on other social media platforms and your website to attract new subscribers.

**Create a consistent posting schedule:** Consistency is key when it comes to building an audience on YouTube. Make sure to post regularly and at optimal times to reach your target audience.

**Engage with your audience:** Engage with your audience by responding to comments and messages, asking questions, and running contests or giveaways.

**Analyze your analytics:** Monitor engagement rates, subscribers growth, type of interactions, total views, etc. Detecting peak times for posting is also vital. You can also identify videos that require replacing or updating.

**Optimize your channel for search with TubeBuddy:**

TubeBuddy is a tool that has become popular among YouTubers for managing their channels and editing their videos. It is 100% safe to use and has been certified by YouTube, so users don't need to worry about their channels being terminated for using it.

TubeBuddy offers a range of services, including SEO, analytics, and video editing tools. The Pro Plan, which starts at $9/month, includes access to tags and keyword research tools, productivity tools, YouTube SEO tools, and video optimization tools. This plan is particularly useful for small channels with less than 1000 subscribers, as TubeBuddy offers a 50% discount on the Pro Plan for these channels.

One of the key features of TubeBuddy is its keyword research tool, which allows users to perform in-depth keyword research and optimize their videos for maximum visibility on YouTube. This feature can save users time and help them earn more from their YouTube channels.

TubeBuddy also offers a range of additional tools and resources for YouTubers, including templates for video titles and descriptions, tools for optimizing video thumbnails, and tools for analyzing the performance of videos.

TubeBuddy is a useful tool for managing and optimizing YouTube channels. Its range of features, including keyword research, video optimization, and analytics, make it a valuable resource for anyone looking to grow their channel and increase their visibility on YouTube.

**TubeBuddy:** https://www.tubebuddy.com/

If you go to OpenAI, https://openai.com/, and sign up for a free Chat GPT account, you can use AI to help you write the perfect YouTube script, with hashtags, using keywords for your industry. Once your account is created, go to the prompt and type in: **Write a YouTube script about (your product or industry)**

**Visit** www.ProspectingHacks.com **for free guides that will help you with your prospecting game plan.**

"THE WILL TO SUCCEED IS IMPORTANT,
BUT WHAT'S MORE IMPORTANT IS
THE WILL TO PREPARE."

-BOBBY KNIGHT

# CREATE A PODCAST

Starting a podcast is a fun and rewarding way to share your ideas and stories with a wider audience, as well as promote your services.

**Here's a step-by-step guide on how to set up your own podcast and get it listed on the major podcasting platforms:**

- **Choose a topic and format for your podcast.** Consider what you're passionate about and what kind of content you want to create. Will your podcast be a solo show, or will you have guests? Will it be a series of interviews, or will you narrate your own stories?
- **Choose a name for your podcast.** Your name should be memorable and reflect the theme and tone of your show.
- **Gather your recording equipment**. You'll need a video camera, a microphone, a mixer, and an audio interface to record your podcast. You can also invest in a pop filter to soften the popping sound when you speak into the microphone.
- **Record and edit your podcast**. Use recording software like Audacity or Adobe Audition to capture your audio and edit your episodes to remove any mistakes or unnecessary segments.
- **Choose a hosting platform for your podcast.** There are several options to choose from, such as anchor.fm, Buzzsprout, and Zencastr. These platforms will provide you with a place to store and distribute your podcast episodes.
- **Submit your podcast to the major podcasting platforms.** This includes Apple Podcasts, Spotify, and Google Podcasts. Each platform has its own submission process, so be sure to follow the guidelines carefully.

- **Promote your podcast.** Use social media, email newsletters, and other marketing channels to promote your podcast and attract new listeners.

**Once your podcast is all set up, invite current and potential clients on to be guests!**

Having your clients as guests on your podcast can offer numerous benefits, including the potential to bring in more business. Here are just a few of the ways that inviting your clients to be on your podcast can help generate new leads and drive growth for your business:

**Increased exposure:**

By inviting your clients to be on your podcast, you can increase your own exposure to their networks and potential customers. When your clients share their appearance on your podcast with their own followers and networks, you can reach a new audience who may be interested in your products or services. This can help increase your visibility and reach and can lead to new leads and potential customers.

**Improved credibility:**

By featuring experts and thought leaders on your podcast, you can improve your own credibility and authority within your industry. This can help establish you as a trusted source of information and a go-to resource for your target audience, which can lead to more interest in your products or services.

**Enhanced content:**

Having your clients as guests on your podcast can also provide a wealth of content for your show. By discussing their expertise and experiences, you can provide valuable insights and information for your listeners. This can help keep your podcast fresh and engaging and can also help attract new listeners who are interested in the topics your clients cover. These new listeners may be potential customers who are interested in your products or services.

**Improved customer loyalty:**

Inviting your clients to be on your podcast can also help improve customer loyalty. By showcasing your clients and demonstrating that you value their contributions, you can create a sense of community and belonging among your listeners. This can help strengthen your relationship with your audience and encourage them to continue listening to your podcast. When your listeners are more loyal and engaged, they are more likely to recommend your products or services to others, which can lead to more business.

**Increased sales:**

Ultimately, having your clients (and potential clients) as guests on your podcast can lead to increased sales. By increasing your exposure, improving your credibility, enhancing your content, and improving customer loyalty, you can create a more favorable environment for generating new leads and closing sales. This can help drive growth and success for your business.

Having your own podcast and inviting your current and potential clients on as guests helps grow your business by increasing exposure, improving credibility, enhancing content, improving customer loyalty, and driving sales. Plus, if you design your interview questions right, your guests will basically tell you step-by-step what they want from a company like yours. Every interview could be a road map to your next big sale!

**Podcast Production Platforms:**

Podcast production platforms are essential tools for hosting, distributing, and promoting your podcast. Here is a review of the top 5 podcast production platforms based on the provided web search results:

**Anchor.fm:** https://anchor.fm/

According to ListenNotes, anchor.fm is the most popular podcast platform, with 49% of podcasts hosted on their platform. It is a simple and user-friendly platform that allows you to easily record, edit, and publish your podcast. It also offers monetization options, such as allowing listeners to make donations or becoming a member of your show.

**Soundcloud:** https://soundcloud.com/

Soundcloud is another popular podcast platform, with 6.4% of podcasts hosted on their platform. It offers a variety of features, including the ability to collaborate with others on your podcast, advanced analytics, and integration with other popular music streaming platforms.

**Buzzsprout:** https://www.buzzsprout.com/

Buzzsprout is a well-respected podcast hosting platform, with approximately 5% of podcasts hosted on their platform. It offers a variety of features, including the ability to schedule your podcast releases, automatic episode publishing to your website, and detailed analytics.

**ZenCastr:** https://zencastr.com/

Zencastr is the ultimate all-in-one podcasting platform. We've bundled all your podcasting needs — record, edit, distribute and monetize all from the same place. It's never been easier to podcast.

**Simplecast:** https://www.simplecast.com/

Simplecast is a powerful podcast hosting platform that is used by some of the biggest names in the industry, such as Medium and Shopify. It offers one-click publishing and their Recast tool for scheduling on social media and podcast websites.

**Podbean:** https://www.podbean.com/

Podbean is another popular podcast hosting platform, with a variety of features including customizable player designs, advanced analytics, and the ability to monetize your podcast through ads and sponsorships.

Overall, each of these podcast production platforms has its own unique set of features and capabilities, so it is important to choose the one that best fits your needs and budget.

**Visit** www.ProspectingHacks.com **for free guides that will help you with your prospecting game plan.**

"EVEN IF YOU'RE ON THE RIGHT TRACK, YOU'LL GET RUN OVER IF YOU JUST SIT THERE."

-WILL ROGERS

 # BE A GUEST ON A PODCAST

If you're looking to score some high-paying clients, you need to let people experience your wisdom firsthand. And what better way to do that than by being a guest on a podcast? With over 2.7 million podcasts out there, there's definitely a show for every kind of expertise. Just make sure you're selling a Rolex to the right audience - you don't want to try and hawk a fancy watch to the mailroom intern.

To get started, find podcasts that welcome guests and that cater to your specific audience. Look for shows that have produced at least 20 recent episodes and have received positive reviews. You can also sign up for online matchmaking sites like PodMatch.com and MatchMaker.fm, or join a Facebook group like Podcast Guest Collaboration Community - Find a Guest, Be a Guest. And don't forget to tap into your own network - there might be people you know who host shows or write columns who would be happy to have you as a guest.

Podcast guesting is all about building lasting business relationships, so don't treat it like a series of one-night stands. Instead, approach it with the mindset that the most important influencer is calling you tomorrow. Be media ready, media savvy, and on message. Prepare a media one sheet that showcases what you have to offer and create an "Interview Me" page that gives hosts everything they need to get up to speed on you and your expertise.

As a sales prospector, having a media kit is an essential tool for promoting your brand and getting invited as a guest on podcasts and other media outlets. A media kit is a collection of information and materials that provide an overview of your business and what you have to offer.

**Here's how to create a media kit for your business that you can use to get on podcasts as a guest:**

**Identify your target audience:**

Before you start creating your media kit, it's important to know who your target audience is and what information they will find most valuable. This will help you tailor your media kit to your audience and make it more effective.

**Gather key information:**

Your media kit should include information about your business, including your mission, goals, and any notable accomplishments. You should also include a bio or company profile, as well as contact information, such as your website, email, and social media profiles.

**Create visuals:**

Visuals are an important part of any media kit, as they help to engage your audience and make your brand more memorable. Consider including a logo, headshot, and any relevant photos or graphics that showcase your business or products.

**Write a press release:**

A press release is a short, written statement that provides information about your business and any notable events or achievements. This can be a useful tool for getting the attention of potential media outlets, including podcasts.

**Assemble the materials:**

Once you have all the necessary information and materials, it's time to assemble your media kit. You can create a physical or digital kit, depending on your needs and preferences. Consider organizing the materials in a way that makes them easy to access and understand.

**Promote your media kit:**

Once you have your media kit created, it's important to promote it to potential media outlets and podcast hosts. You can do this by sharing your media kit on your website, social media profiles, and other relevant online platforms. You can also send your media kit directly to media outlets and podcast hosts that you are interested in working with.

By creating a media kit and promoting it to potential media outlets, you can increase your chances of being invited as a guest on a podcast and share your expertise with a large and engaged audience. A media kit is an essential tool for any business looking to promote itself and reach a wider audience.

Once you've gained some experience and confidence through the matchmaking sites, you might be ready to take on bigger shows with more influential hosts. Reach out to the influencers you admire, do your research on their shows, and suggest a unique point of view that would add value to their audience. With these tips, you'll be well on your way to attracting more high-paying clients through podcast guesting.

**Here is a sample email you could send to request to be a podcast guest:**

Dear [Host's Name],

My name is [Your Name] and I am a [Your Job Title/Company] based in [City/State]. I am writing to introduce myself as a potential guest on your podcast, [Podcast Name].

I believe that my experiences and expertise make me a unique and valuable contributor to your show. As a freelancer, I understand the importance of strong writing skills and would love the opportunity to share my insights and advice with your audience.

I have taken the time to listen to a recent episode of your podcast, [Name of Episode], and was particularly interested in the discussion on [Topic]. I feel that my own experiences and perspective on this topic would add value to your show and provide valuable insights to your listeners.

I have attached a brief bio and links to some of my relevant work for your consideration. I would be honored to be a guest on your podcast and contribute to the important discussions you are having.

Thank you for considering my request. I look forward to the opportunity to share my thoughts and experiences with your audience.

Sincerely, [Your Name]

 **FROM THE FIELD**

This has more impact if you do a video email.

 **AI TIP**

If you go to OpenAI, https://openai.com/, and sign up for a free ChatGPT account, you can use AI to help you write the perfect podcast guest email using keywords for your industry. After you create the account, go to the prompt and type in: **Write an email requesting for me to be a guest on a podcast about _____**

"THE MAN WHO DOES MORE THAN HE IS PAID FOR WILL SOON BE PAID FOR MORE THAN HE DOES."

-NAPOLEON HILL

# AI CHAT BOTS

Artificial intelligence (AI) chatbots can be a powerful tool for sales prospecting. These chatbots use machine learning algorithms to communicate with potential customers in a natural and personalized way on your website, providing a convenient and efficient way for businesses to reach out to prospects and qualify leads.

**There are several ways that AI chatbots can be used for sales prospecting:**

**Providing real-time sales and marketing communication:**

Chatbots can be used to engage with potential customers in real-time, providing information about products and services and answering questions. This can be especially effective for businesses that operate in a fast-moving market or have a large volume of potential customers.

**Qualifying leads:**

One strategy for using chatbots to qualify leads is to ask relevant questions. This can include gathering information about a customer's budget, decision-making process, and timeline for purchasing. Chatbots can also help schedule appointments, which is particularly useful for B2B firms and healthcare organizations that receive a high volume of meeting requests.

**Scheduling appointments:**

Chatbots can be used to schedule appointments with potential customers, streamlining the sales process and reducing the need for manual scheduling.

**Providing personalized recommendations:**

AI chatbots can analyze customer data and provide personalized recommendations, helping businesses tailor their sales pitch and increase the likelihood of a sale.

To use AI chatbots for sales prospecting, businesses need to first identify the specific goals they want to achieve and then choose a chatbot platform that meets their needs. Some popular options include **Drift**, **VideoAsk**, **ManyChat**, and **MobileMonkey**. Once the chatbot is set up, businesses can use it to engage with potential customers and gather valuable insights that can help them refine their sales strategy and improve their chances of success.

AI chatbots can gather relevant information about a potential customer's preferences and needs through conversational insights, allowing businesses to gain insight into the customer's experience and determine if they are a qualified lead.

It's important to remember that chatbots are interacting with real people, so it's important to treat them with respect and not like a "moron." Chatbots should be designed to provide a positive customer experience and gather relevant information in a respectful and professional manner.

Chatbots should be able to recognize the difference between a lead and a viable prospect (a lead with true potential to become a customer). This means that the chatbot should be able to ask qualifying questions that help determine whether a lead is worth pursuing.

The chatbot might start by asking the prospect about their needs and goals. For example, the chatbot might ask: "Tell me what you're looking for to get the most out of this product or service." This will help the chatbot understand whether the prospect's needs align with what the business has to offer.

In addition to asking about the prospect's needs, the chatbot might also ask about the prospect's engagement level. This could involve questions about how interested the prospect is in the product or service, or how likely they are to make a purchase.

The qualifying questions that a chatbot should ask will depend on the specific goals and needs of the business. However, some general questions that might be useful for identifying new sales leads include:

- What are you looking to achieve with this product or service?
- How interested are you in making a purchase?
- What are your main concerns or questions about this product or service?
- Can you tell me more about your current situation and how this product or service might fit in?

**Here is a breakdown of the prospect information flow a chatbot might be set up to do:**

**Step 1: Greet the customer and introduce the chatbot.**

The chatbot should start the conversation by greeting the customer and introducing itself. This can be done by saying something like "Hello, I'm [chatbot name], a virtual assistant here to help you. How can I assist you today?"

**Step 2: Ask for the customer's name and contact information.**

The chatbot should ask for the customer's name and contact information, such as their email address and phone number. This can be done by saying something like "To better assist you, may I have your name and contact information?"

**Step 3: Collect information about the customer's needs and preferences.**

The chatbot should ask the customer about their specific needs and preferences. This can include questions about what products or services they are interested in, their budget, and any specific features they are looking for.

**Step 4: Provide personalized recommendations.**

Based on the information gathered in steps 2 and 3, the chatbot should provide personalized recommendations to the customer. This can include specific products or services that match their needs and preferences, as well as any special deals or promotions that may be of interest to them.

**Step 5: Schedule a follow-up call or appointment.**

Once the customer has received the recommended products or services, the chatbot should schedule a follow-up call or appointment with the customer to ensure they are satisfied with their purchase. This can be done by saying something like "Would you like to schedule a call with one of our representatives to follow up on your purchase?"

**Step 6: Collect feedback.**

Lastly, the chatbot should collect feedback from the customer about their experience with the chatbot and the products or services they received. This can be done by asking a series of questions about the customer's satisfaction and whether or not they would recommend the company to others.

AI chatbots can be a valuable tool for sales prospecting, providing businesses with a convenient and efficient way to reach out to potential customers and qualify leads. By leveraging the power of machine learning algorithms, businesses can improve their sales process and increase their chances of success.

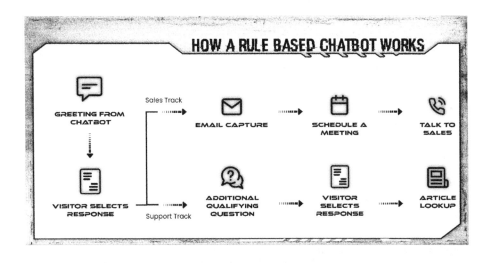

## Text Chatbot Platforms:

Drift:            https://www.drift.com/
ManyChat:         https://manychat.com/
MobileMonkey:     https://mobilemonkey.com/

## Video Chat Bot:

VideoAsk:   https://www.videoask.com/

"BE CAREFUL HOW YOU ARE TALKING TO YOURSELF BECAUSE YOU ARE LISTENING."

-LISA M. HAYES

# IN-PERSON PROSPECTING

# REFERRALS

According to a recent online survey, 68% of sales professionals believe that referrals from existing customers offer the best leads for B2B prospecting. This makes sense, since prospects are often more receptive to recommendations from other industry peers or colleagues, as they're perceived as being more trustworthy and having a lack of agenda compared to salespeople.

However, in the real world, customer referrals don't just happen magically. To get your satisfied customers to refer your solution to others, you need to offer an exceptional product and provide excellent customer service. And even with that foundation in place, you still need to actively connect with your happy customers and ask for referrals. Don't worry, this doesn't have to be super intimidating – just casually include friendly requests and reminders when you check in with customers to see how they're enjoying your solution.

# FROM THE FIELD

Video email is amazing for all of these tips.

**Offer excellent customer service:**

Satisfied customers are more likely to refer others to your business. Make sure to exceed their expectations and deliver high-quality products or services.

**Show appreciation for your customers:**

A simple thank you or gesture of appreciation can go a long way in building trust and encouraging customers to refer others to your business.

**Make it easy for customers to refer others:**

Consider creating a referral program or providing referral cards or other materials that make it easy for customers to refer others to your business.

**Personalize your ask:**

Instead of a generic request for referrals, tailor your ask to individual customers. Consider their interests, values, and the specific ways in which your business has helped them.

**Follow up with customers who have made referrals:**

Show your appreciation by thanking them and offering a special discount or other reward. This can help strengthen your relationship and encourage them to refer more customers in the future.

**Stay connected with customers who have not yet made referrals:**

By maintaining regular contact and building a strong relationship, you can create an opportunity to ask for referrals in the future.

The easiest (and coolest) way I have found to ask for referrals is with Video Email. Create a video email asking your current customer for a referral. In the video ask them just to "Reply With Video". All they have to do is hit the "Reply With Video" button on the email you sent, say something nice about you for 30 seconds, and hit send. Moments of their time, but lots of extra future dollars for you!

By consistently generating referrals from satisfied customers, you can build a strong base of leads that will make your B2B prospecting efforts more effective and efficient. And let's be honest, who doesn't want that?

So go ahead and ask your customers for referrals – it'll be a win-win for both of you.

 **FROM THE FIELD**

I stopped to get gas. I had to catch a flight to Austin, and I was already late running last minute errands. Standing next to my car, about to choose what octane I needed, I look over at the gas station right when this kid comes up to me holding a bundle of wood (I'm sure a bundle of wood has a proper name, but I don't know what it is.) He asks me if I would like to buy some wood. I look back at the gas station from where he came from and all along the wall of the side of the gas station is all of this chopped wood. This is Houston, Texas. I live in the middle of the city. Why do I need wood? I told the kid no, but as he was walking away, I asked him, "where did you get all of that wood?" Just seemed odd this kid has all this chopped wood piled up at a gas station.

He starts telling me this story about his grandfather, and how he has a chopped wood business. He sells his wood to all the local Italian and Pizza restaurants for their wood fired pizza. I ask him more about his grandfather and he ends up telling me that once every week the two of them drive around and personally take orders. They spend 1-2 days a week driving to all of their customers to see if they need wood that week. Any wood they didn't sell, his grandfather piles up at the gas station and the kid tries to sell it to people getting gas. Why they just don't take it back home, I have no idea. But that's what they were doing, and it seemed to be working. It wasn't long before I knew why.

The kid tells me that the part of Houston I live in has a lot of nice, upper boulevard homes – and a lot of people have their own wood ovens in the back yard. When those people get gas, they pick up some wood for their backyard pizza oven. The kid starts telling me how they always sell out after they deliver orders to the restaurants. I find this whole story amazing, and I also find the entire process laborious and expensive.

There are so many easier, more efficient ways to sell this wood. I feel a project, I can smell it!

I ask the kid if I could talk to his grandfather. The kid pulls out a cell phone and calls him (a referral!), hands me the phone. I Introduce myself and give him my elevator pitch. I explain to him how if he had a website where his customers could just order what they needed online he would not only make more money but save a ton of money and time (as well as he wouldn't have to leave his grandson hocking wood at a gas station), driving around to each customer guessing what they might want every week. "Can I come talk to you right now so we can get this situation fixed as soon as possible?" I ask. Then I wait. "Ya, come on by, let's talk about this." The kid gives me the address to their "wood farm". I call Southwest Airlines, get my ticket changed, I've got to help this family sell more wood – it's my destiny!

I get to the address, and I am now in some part of Houston I have never been to before. Nothing but grass fields. The address is a mailbox on a dirt road. I go down the dirt road (no trees, just grass fields everywhere) until I see a pickup truck with this old man, like really, really old man sitting on the tailgate. The back of the truck is full of wood, I must be close! I get out of my car and ask if he's _____. He says yes and invites me to have a seat. I was at the gas station on my way to the airport to have dinner with friends, and in an instant, I am now sitting in a tall grass field with some very old man I have never met before talking about how to sell wood online.

I had some Post-Its in my car. I grab them and a pen and I draw out sitting on his tailgate how this could work. His new **online wood supply business model**! He pauses as he looks at the now botched together string of Post-Its I have created. He says, "I like it. But what I like most about it is I can be with my grandson more instead of him being at that gas station." He gave me the most amazing smile anyone has ever given me. I still can't believe what is going on.

"How long and how much?" He asked very confidently, as if he could care less. I looked down at the Post-Its, "I need about three weeks to design and program everything, my firm charges (at the time) $5,000 a week, instead of $15,000, let's just make it an even $10,000 and I will throw in a video of you and your grandson to have on the home page and YouTube." He looks at me for a moment... and I am not kidding, he reaches in his pocket and pulls out a wad of $100's. Counts out $10k and hands it to me. No contract, no paperwork of any kind. Just two guys sitting on the back of a wood truck in a grass field at the end of the day. I assure him of the process, and how I am a big fan of transparency and communication and that I would be back in 2-3 days with a mock-up of what it would look like.

He shakes my hand, pats me on the shoulder and looks up at me and says, "That's all fine, but what is YouTube?". I just smile and tell him I'll show him when it's done, but it's going to be amazing for business. He shakes my hand one last time, gets in his wood truck and drives off, leaving me standing in the middle of a tall grass field holding $10k in cash, on a hot Houston afternoon.

I go back to my car and my engine won't start. I got so excited, I never got gas! I call Lexus roadside, tell them where I'm at. They ask why I was in the middle of tall grass field with my Lexus and no gas. I just told them they wouldn't believe it.

**True Story.**

"TREAT YOUR CUSTOMERS AS THOUGH YOU
WERE THEIR MOST DEDICATED EMPLOYEE
AND CONSULTANT, READY TO SERVE THEM
IN EVERY WAY, SO THEY FEEL YOUR COMPANY
IS PRACTICALLY A DIVISION OF
THEIR COMPANY."

-HARVEY MACKAY

# HOST AN INDUSTRY EVENT

Hosting an industry event can be a great way to generate new business prospects and clients for your company. These events provide an opportunity to showcase your expertise and thought leadership within your industry, as well as to network with other professionals and potential partners. By hosting a successful industry event, you can not only attract new business, but also establish your company as a leader in your field.

**Here are a few key points to consider when hosting an industry event:**

**Determine your goals:**

Before you start planning your event, it's important to identify what you hope to achieve. Do you want to generate leads, showcase your products or services, or simply network with other professionals in your industry? Clearly defining your goals will help you tailor your event to meet your specific needs and ensure that you get the most out of it.

**Choose the right format:**

There are many different formats that you can use for your industry event, including conferences, workshops, seminars, and networking events. Choose the format that best fits your goals and target audience.

**Select a suitable venue:**

Consider the size, location, and amenities of the venue when selecting a place to host your event. You'll also want to think about the accessibility of the venue and whether it has the necessary facilities to accommodate your needs.

**Promote your event:**

Use a variety of marketing channels to promote your event and attract attendees. This can include social media, email marketing, and traditional media outlets. Consider offering early bird discounts or other incentives to encourage people to register early.

**Engage your attendees:**

Once you have people registered for your event, it's important to keep them engaged and interested. This can be achieved through a variety of ways, such as offering interactive sessions or networking opportunities, providing high-quality content, and ensuring that your speakers are knowledgeable and engaging.

**Follow up after the event:**

After your event is over, be sure to follow up with attendees and thank them for their participation. This is a great opportunity to nurture relationships and potentially turn attendees into clients or business partners.

Hosting an industry event can be a lot of work, but it can also be a highly effective way to generate new business prospects and clients for your company. By planning and executing a successful event, you can establish your company as a thought leader in your industry and create valuable opportunities for growth and success.

"YOU CAN MAKE MORE FRIENDS
IN TWO MONTHS BY BEING INTERESTED
IN THEM THAN IN TWO YEARS BY
MAKING THEM INTERESTED IN YOU."

-DALE CARNEGIE

# BE A GUEST SPEAKER AT AN INDUSTRY EVENT

Being a guest speaker at an industry event or luncheon can provide numerous benefits for your business and can be a valuable tool for sales prospecting. Here are some ways in which being a guest speaker can help with sales prospecting:

Establishing credibility and expertise: By speaking at an industry event, you have the opportunity to showcase your knowledge and expertise on a particular topic. This can help to establish you as a thought leader in your industry and can increase credibility for your business.

**Reaching a new audience:**

Industry events and luncheons often attract attendees from a variety of companies and organizations. By speaking at one of these events, you have the opportunity to reach a new audience and introduce your business to potential customers who may not have otherwise been aware of you.

**Building relationships:**

Speaking at an industry event or luncheon allows you to interact with attendees and engage with them on a personal level. This can be an effective way to build relationships with potential customers and establish trust, which can ultimately lead to increased sales.

**Generating leads:**

By including a call-to-action (CTA) in your presentation or by networking with attendees after your talk, you can generate leads for your business.

This can be especially effective if you have a product or service that is relevant to the topic you are speaking about.

 **AI TIP**

If you go to OpenAI, https://openai.com/, and sign up for a free Chat GPT account, you can use AI to help you write the perfect guest speaker script using keywords for your industry. Once your account is created, go to the prompt and type in: **Write an outline for a guest speaker talking about (your industry)**

**Improving SEO:**

If the event or luncheon is being promoted online, there may be opportunities for your business to be mentioned in the promotional materials. This can improve the visibility of your business and help to improve your search engine optimization (SEO), making it easier for potential customers to find you.

Being a guest speaker at an industry event or luncheon can provide numerous benefits for your business and can be a valuable tool for sales prospecting. By showcasing your expertise, reaching a new audience, building relationships, generating leads, and potentially improving your SEO, you can increase visibility for your business and potentially generate leads.

**Guest Speaker Agencies:**

AAE                     https://www.allamericanspeakers.com/
Lavin                  https://www.thelavinagency.com/
National Speakers Bureau https://www.nsb.com/

"DO WHAT YOU CAN, WITH WHAT YOU HAVE, WHERE YOU ARE."

-WILLIAM MEEK WIDENER

 # MIND YOUR SURROUNDINGS

As a sales professional, it's important to always be on the lookout for potential new clients. And while it's easy to focus on traditional methods of prospecting, such as networking events or cold calls, there are also plenty of opportunities to find new leads in your everyday life. Here are some examples of how to prospect for new clients by paying attention to your surroundings:

**At church:**

If you attend church regularly, take the opportunity to strike up a conversation with someone new. You never know, they may be in need of your products or services, or know someone who is.

**At a game:**

Whether it's a baseball game or a local soccer match, there are likely plenty of people in attendance who could potentially be interested in your products or services. Take the time to introduce yourself and see if there are any leads worth pursuing.

**At a bar:**

While it may seem unconventional, a bar can be a great place to meet new people and potentially find new clients. Just be sure to approach the conversation in a professional manner, and always remember to have a business card on hand.

**At the mall:**

Whether you're shopping or just passing through, the mall is a great place to meet new people and potentially find new clients. Look for opportunities to strike up a conversation and see if there are any leads worth pursuing.

**At a community event:**

From farmers markets to local festivals, there are plenty of community events that can be great places to find new clients. Take the time to introduce yourself and see if there are any leads worth pursuing.

By paying attention to your surroundings and being open to opportunities, you may be able to find new clients in unexpected places. Just make sure to always be professional and respectful in your interactions and follow up with any potential leads.

 **FROM THE FIELD**

I was on a flight from JFK to Zurich, and since it was a long flight, I treated myself to first class. Once settled in by the window with my eyes already shut, I was disturbed by the movement of someone sitting next to me. Halfway sitting up, it was a lady who clearly was a businesswoman (her outfit, her demeanor, etc.). She made a comment "lucky devil, you got the window." Even though it was assigned seating, I got her point. I sat up and insisted she take it. After a few moments of polite banter, she took me up on my offer.

Settling back down, she asked me why I was going to Zurich. At this point in my life, I spent two weeks every summer racing MonoRacers, https://www.peravescz.com/, from Zurich to Byrno (a small town south of Prague with an amazing racetrack). We would start in Zurich, race to Byrno down the Autobahn, spend time racing the track in Byrno, then race back to Zurich. I did this for about 4 years. I was on my way to test my immortality once more.

I asked her why she was going, and she mentioned she was going to shop for Rolex watches for her husband for their anniversary, he was going to meet her there. My ears perked up. Little did she know I happened to be wearing, (and still wear to this day) what is called a Zenith Patrizzi Stainless Steel Daytona Rolex. An impossible watch to find (how I got mine, brand new, at cost, is a different book.)

For the rest of the flight, I shared my knowledge of what to look for with the different styles of Rolex's on the market, as well as I feathered in all the field production adventures my Rolex had gone through on different projects I had produced all over the world. At the end of the flight, she thanked me for the insight, and gave me her card. Four months later we connected again, and I ended producing a media package for her company for $350,000.

"BEGIN SOMEWHERE;
YOU CANNOT BUILD A REPUTATION ON
WHAT YOU INTEND TO DO."

-LIZ SMITH

# ALTERNATIVE PROSPECTING

# AFFILIATE MARKETING

Affiliate marketing is a performance-based marketing strategy in which a business rewards affiliates (pays you cash) for each customer brought about by the affiliate's own marketing efforts. The business pays a commission to the affiliates (you) for each sale or lead that is generated because of the marketing efforts of the affiliates. In other words, sign up for an affiliate link, distribute that link across your online footprint, and then every time someone clicks on the link you provided and buys something from your affiliate partner that partner pays you – 24x7.

Affiliate marketing is a way for businesses to reach new customers by partnering with individuals or companies that already have an established online presence and a proven track record of driving traffic and sales. These affiliates promote the business's products or services in exchange for a commission on each sale or lead that they generate.

There are several ways that affiliates can use affiliate marketing for sales prospecting and automating their marketing efforts. Here are a few examples:

1. Affiliates can use email marketing to reach out to potential customers and promote the business's products or services. By using email marketing software, affiliates can automate their email campaigns and send targeted emails to potential customers based on their interests and demographics.
2. Affiliates can use social media marketing to promote the business's products or services to their followers. By using social media scheduling tools, affiliates can automate their social media posts and reach a larger audience with minimal effort.

3. Affiliates can use content marketing to promote the business's products or services through blog posts, articles, and other forms of online content. By creating valuable, informative content, affiliates can attract potential customers and drive traffic to the business's website.

4. Affiliates can use search engine optimization (SEO) techniques to optimize their websites and improve their search engine rankings. By optimizing their websites for specific keywords, affiliates can increase the chances of their websites ranking highly in search engine results and attracting potential customers.

# Affiliate Marketing Case Study: NerdWallet

NerdWallet is a personal finance company that helps consumers make informed decisions about credit cards, loans, and other financial products. One of the ways that NerdWallet generates revenue is through affiliate marketing.

The company partners with financial institutions and credit card companies and pays affiliates a commission for each sale or lead generated as a result of their marketing efforts.

**For example, let's say that an affiliate promotes a credit card on their website. If a visitor to the website clicks on the credit card link and subsequently applies for and is approved for the credit card, the affiliate will earn a commission from NerdWallet for the sale.**

NerdWallet uses a variety of marketing tactics to promote its financial products and services to consumers. The company has a large team of writers and researchers who create educational content about personal finance, including blog posts, articles, and videos. This content is designed to help consumers make informed decisions about their finances and may include links to financial products or services that NerdWallet promotes as an affiliate.

In addition to creating educational content, NerdWallet also uses search engine optimization (SEO) techniques to improve the visibility of its website in search engine results. By optimizing its website for specific keywords, NerdWallet can increase the chances that its website will rank highly in search results and attract potential customers.

NerdWallet's use of affiliate marketing is a key part of the company's business model. By partnering with financial institutions and credit card companies and promoting their products to consumers, NerdWallet is able to generate revenue and help consumers make informed decisions about their finances.

You can find affiliate marketing information usually in the footer of any website you wish to promote. You can also join, for free, affiliate marketing platforms that give you thousands of affiliate links you can use in your social media posts, newsletters, YouTube video descriptions, and even in your email footer!

**Here is a list of some of the most popular affiliate marketing platforms:**

| | |
|---|---|
| ClickBank | https://www.clickbank.com/ |
| Commission Junction | https://www.cj.com/ |
| ShareASale | https://www.shareasale.com/info/ |
| PartnerStack | https://partnerstack.com/ |

Affiliate marketing is a valuable strategy for businesses looking to expand their customer base and increase their sales. By partnering with affiliates who have an established online presence and a proven track record of driving traffic and sales, businesses can reach new customers and automate their marketing efforts to generate more leads and sales.

# SNAIL MAIL

Go old school (and stand out from your competitors) and send a sales letter through the mail! When do you think the last time a prospect got a personal, or even hand written, letter in the mail? A sales letter is a written sales tool that is designed to persuade the reader to take a specific action, such as purchasing a product or service. To be effective, a sales letter should include a number of important features. Here are some key elements of a successful sales letter:

## A clear and compelling subject line:

The subject line of a sales letter is the first thing the reader will see, and it needs to be clear and compelling to grab their attention and encourage them to keep reading. A good subject line should be specific, relevant, and benefit-oriented, and it should entice the reader to want to learn more.

## A strong opening:

The opening of a sales letter is crucial for capturing the reader's attention and setting the stage for the rest of the letter. A strong opening should be engaging, benefit-oriented, and relevant to the reader's needs and interests. It should also clearly state the purpose of the letter and what the reader can expect to learn.

## A clear and compelling value proposition:

A value proposition is a statement that clearly explains the benefits and value of your product or service to the reader. It should be clear, concise, and compelling, and it should convince the reader that your offering is worth their time and investment.

**Evidence and credibility:**

To convince the reader to take action, it's important to provide evidence and credibility to support your claims. This can include testimonials from satisfied customers, data or research, and examples of how your product or service has helped others.

**A sense of urgency:**

Creating a sense of urgency can help motivate the reader to take action now rather than waiting. This can be achieved through limited time offers, bonuses for early adopters, or a limited supply of the product or service.

**A clear call to action:**

A call to action is a specific request that tells the reader what they should do next. It should be clear, concise, and actionable, and it should be prominently placed in the letter. Some examples of calls to action could include "Buy now," "Sign up today," or "Learn more."

**A strong closing:**

The closing of a sales letter is the final opportunity to persuade the reader to take action. A strong closing should summarize the benefits of the product or service, restate the call to action, and provide a sense of what the reader can expect after taking action.

Sales letters can be an effective tool for generating leads, as long as they are used correctly. I have personally used sales letters in my own business and have written them for my clients as well. Through my experience, I have learned a few key things about getting a good response to sales letters:

**Use a highly targeted list of ideal prospects.** This will increase the chances of getting a good response.

**A two-page letter tends to be more effective than a shorter letter.** While it may go against the current wisdom that people don't read more than a page, I have found that a two-page letter works well, particularly for B2B clients.

A letter that looks and reads like an actual letter, rather than a polished marketing piece, tends to be more effective.

**Including a small physical item in the letter, like a stylus pen, can increase the chances of it being opened.** However, the freebie or gimmick often gets all the attention, and the prospect may not read the letter. It's better to focus on writing a great sales letter that stands on its own merits.

**Don't force the prospect to reply only through a website landing page.** Offer the option to call or email as well, as responses via phone or email tend to come from higher-quality prospects.

There are many other tips and tricks for creating a marketing letter that brings in business, but these are just a few key points to consider. If you're not currently using sales letters to reach out to prospects, it may be worth giving them a try as a supplement to your other lead-generating methods.

A successful sales letter should include a clear and compelling subject line, a strong opening, a clear and compelling value proposition, evidence and credibility, a sense of urgency, a clear call to action, and a strong closing. By including these key elements, you can effectively persuade the reader to take the desired action and drive sales for your business.

 **AI TIP**

If you go to OpenAI, https://openai.com/, and sign up for a free Chat GPT account, you can use AI to help you write the perfect snail mail sales letter using keywords for your industry. Once your account is created, go to the prompt and type in: **Write an introductory sales letter about (your industry)**

**Visit www.ProspectingHacks.com for free guides that will help you with your prospecting game plan.**

## Sample Sales Letter 1:

Your Letterhead Stationery
Date
Your Client's Address

Dear _____,

As summer approaches, we understand that you may be looking for ways to keep your office cool and comfortable for you and your colleagues. That's why we have developed room coolers in a range of capacities to meet your needs. Our enclosed pamphlet provides detailed specifications for our products, as well as a guarantee of five years against all manufacturing defects. We are also offering to repair or replace any part that causes trouble at our own cost.

To help you determine the best location for our coolers in your office, we have included a card with the pamphlet for you to fill out and mail back to us, or feel free to reach out to us via our website at www.yoursite.com. One of our technicians will then visit your office to inspect your space and suggest the most appropriate placement of the coolers to maintain a comfortable temperature throughout the summer.

If you place your order before July 30th, we are offering a special discount of 5%. Our team will also transport and install the coolers at your convenience, free of charge.

We believe that you will find this special offer to be an excellent opportunity to keep your office comfortable and efficient during the hot summer months. Thank you for considering our products.

Sincerely,

Your Name

## Sample Sales Letter 2:

**Enviro-Clean Gets Your House Sparkling Clean and Helps the Environment**
**\*\*Your Business Logo Here\*\***

Your Letterhead Stationery

Date

Your Client's Address

Dear _____,

*For just $150, you can have a clean and sparkling home without exposing yourself or your family to harmful chemical cleaners. At* **Enviro-Clean***, we prioritize the environment and use only state-of-the-art green cleaning methods to ensure your safety. Some benefits of choosing* **Enviro-Clean** *include:*

*Non-toxic cleaning products that are safe for children and pets*
*Clean, sparkling, and hygienic surfaces*
*Bonded and fully insured staff*
*Senior discounts for those aged 65 and over*

*Our satisfaction guarantee means that if you are not happy with our service, we will make it right. Many of our customers have praised our top-notch cleaning job at a reasonable price and have been amazed by our ability to get things clean and sparkling without using toxic chemicals.*

*To get a free estimate, call us at 555-555-5555, or email us at* info@enviro-clean.com. *Make your home clean and contribute to the protection of the environment with* **Enviro-Clean***.*

*Sincerely,*

Your Name
Enviro-Clean Inc.

**P.S.** We are offering a 10% discount for first time users of our service until the end of the year.

## Sample Sales Letter 3:

Your Letterhead Stationery
Date
Your Client's Address

Dear Client,

If you're looking for an accurate and affordable bookkeeping service for your clients, look no further than Bookkeepers *NOW*. If you feel like you're spending too much time on low-level tasks and would rather focus on more challenging and strategic accounting and tax issues with your clients, let us take the bookkeeping burden off your hands. We offer a range of services, including:

Full-service bookkeeping for small businesses using QuickBooks software of all versions and editions

Over 12 years of experience in bookkeeping for small and medium-sized businesses

A staff of 100% Certified QuickBooks ProAdvisors and Microsoft Excel experts

A money-back satisfaction guarantee

We have experience working with clients in a variety of industries, including restaurants, construction, healthcare, professional services, and retail. We can work for you (you take a markup and bill the client) or directly for the client (we will pay you a referral fee), whichever you prefer. References are available for your review.

If you want to reduce your paperwork and improve your clients' bookkeeping experience, don't hesitate to call us today to discuss how we can work together for mutual benefit.

Sincerely,

Bookkeeper

"OFTEN, IN THE REAL WORLD,
IT'S NOT THE SMART WHO GET AHEAD
BUT THE BOLD."

-ROBERT T. KIYOSAKI

 # AUTOMATED POSTCARDS

This kind of goes along with Snail Mail - **with a twist**.

Automating the process of sending personalized, hand-written follow-up postcards and messages to prospects is a huge differentiator from your competition and can be a powerful tool for businesses looking to increase sales and build relationships with potential customers. By offering a bonus or incentive for prospects who call back after filling out a form on your website, LinkedIn page, or landing page, you can increase the chances of making a successful sale.

To make the message seem more personal and draw the prospect's attention, consider using different handwriting styles that vary in pen pressure and line angle changes, or incorporate the use of glyphs. You can also set up a schedule for sending postcards, such as holidays, birthdays, work anniversaries, or as part of a drip sequence over time. In addition to postcards, you can also send out notecards, letters, and gift cards.

One way to enhance the impact of your postcards is to include a QR code that links back to a landing page or website with more information about your services. This can provide prospects with an easy way to learn more about your business and make it easier for them to make a purchase decision.

What I do with my landing pages is connect handwritten postcards to my online forms. The way this works is, when a website visitor fills out one of my forms for a promotion I might be doing, the form will also trigger a handwritten postcard they will get in a week or so. That postcard might have other offers, a QR code that leads to a sales funnel, or a "Godfather Offer" that makes them spend more money with me. If you are interested in setting up this kind of automation, go to www.ProspectingHacks.com and book one of my Ultimate Landing Page Automation packages.

Overall, automating the process of sending personalized, hand-written follow-up postcards and messages can be a powerful tool for businesses looking to increase sales and build relationships with potential customers. By offering incentives, incorporating personal touches, and providing additional information through QR codes, you can increase the chances of making a successful sale.

**The service I use for this is Thanks.io:** www.thanks.io

"THERE ARE TWO WAYS TO GET
TO THE TOP OF AN OAK TREE.
ONE WAY IS TO SIT ON AN ACORN AND WAIT;
THE OTHER WAY IS TO CLIMB IT."

-KEMMONS WILSON

# WRITE A BOOK

Writing a book can be a powerful tool for sales prospecting and building your brand as an expert in your field. Here are a few ways that publishing a book can help you attract new clients and close more sales:

**Establish your expertise:**

Writing a book requires a lot of research, knowledge, and dedication. By publishing a book, you are demonstrating to potential clients that you are an expert in your field and have valuable insights to share. This can make you stand out from the competition and give you credibility in the eyes of prospects.

**Position yourself as a thought leader:**

A book can help you position yourself as a thought leader in your industry. By sharing your ideas and expertise through a book, you can establish yourself as a go-to source for information and inspiration in your field. This can make you more attractive to potential clients who are looking for guidance from a trusted authority.

**Build your personal brand:**

A book can be a powerful marketing tool for building your personal brand. By publishing a book, you can create a strong and consistent message about who you are and what you stand for. This can help you attract clients who align with your values and vision.

**Increase your visibility:**

A book can help increase your visibility and reach a wider audience. When you publish a book, you have the opportunity to promote it through various channels, such as social media, newsletters, and speaking engagements. This can help you attract new clients and build your network.

**Provide value to prospects:**

A book can be a valuable resource for prospects who are considering working with you. By providing valuable information and insights through a book, you can show potential clients the value that you can provide and how you can help them solve their problems.

To maximize the impact of your book for sales prospecting, it's important to choose a topic that is relevant and valuable to your target audience. Consider their pain points and needs, and focus on how you can provide solutions and value through your book.

In addition to writing a high-quality book, it's important to promote it effectively to reach your target audience. This can include using social media, email marketing, and speaking engagements to share your book and its message with potential clients.

**Think of your book as the first step in your sales funnel:**

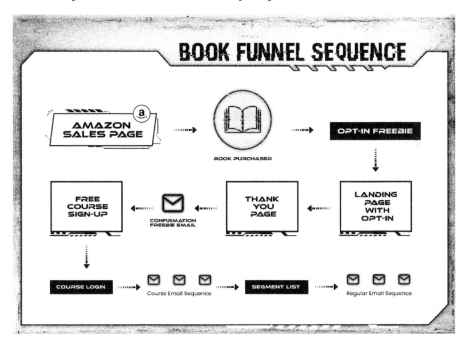

A business book can be an effective tool for creating a sales funnel. A sales funnel is a marketing strategy that involves attracting and nurturing leads through a series of steps, with the goal of converting them into customers. A business book can be used to attract leads and guide them through the funnel, ultimately leading to a sale.

One way to use a business book as a sales funnel is to offer a free copy of the book in exchange for contact information, such as an email address. Once the lead has provided their contact information, they can be added to a mailing list, where they will receive additional information about the author's products or services. This is the first step in the funnel, known as the "awareness" stage, where the goal is to attract potential customers.

As the lead continues to engage with the author's content, they will learn more about the author's expertise and the benefits of their products or services. This is the second step in the funnel, known as the "consideration" stage, where the goal is to educate and nurture the lead. This can be done through a series of email campaigns or webinars, which build on the information presented in the book.

As the lead becomes more interested in the author's products or services, they may be offered a free trial or consultation. This is the third step in the funnel, known as the "conversion" stage, where the goal is to turn the lead into a customer.

Finally, once the lead has become a customer, they can be encouraged to leave a review of the book and share their experience with others. This is the final step in the funnel, known as the "loyalty" stage, where the goal is to keep the customer coming back.

However, it's important to keep in mind that this is just one way a business book can be used as a sales funnel. A well-written business book can also be used to establish the author as a thought leader in their industry, attract media attention and speaking opportunities, or be used as a marketing tool to generate leads in a trade show or event. The importance here is that the book has a consistent messaging with the rest of the marketing material, it's well-written and engaging and the audience is clearly defined.

A business book can be a powerful tool in the sales funnel process, helping to attract leads and guide them through the funnel to a sale. By offering a free copy of the book in exchange for contact information, providing valuable information and building trust and credibility, an author can effectively convert leads into customers. However, it's important to consider the book holistically, how it fits in with the rest of the marketing and sales strategy, to be able to maximize the use of the book as a sales funnel.

**Once your book is written, check out Book Funnel.com**: https://bookfunnel.com/

**Steps To Creating and Promoting Your Book:**

**Step 1: Before You Start Writing**

Before starting to write your book, it is important to have a clear understanding of the purpose and goals of your book. The first step is to identify the reason(s) for writing the book, whether it is to use as a marketing tool, to offer for sale, or to give away as a business card or sales brochure.

Next, determine the primary problem that your book will solve in the marketplace. This could be helping people overcome rejections to increase sales, managing time better to increase productivity, or terminating employees correctly to avoid lawsuits, etc.

Identify the target audience for your book, the people who have the problem that your book solves. This could be salespeople, HR managers, CEOs, or the general public.

Research the existing books in your subject area to gauge the marketplace. Develop a working title for your book that grabs attention, and a working subtitle that clarifies the meaning of the title and explains the benefits of reading the book.

It's also important to gauge interest from the target audience before you start the writing process. Run your book idea past 5-10 targeted buyers to gauge their general level of interest. If the interest is low, it's best to consider a different topic.

After you have completed these steps, make a decision on whether this is the book you want to commit to writing. If the answer is yes, proceed to the actual process of writing. If the answer is no, consider finding another topic idea.

**Step 2: Writing Your Book**

When writing your book, it's important to have a clear plan and structure in place. As a general rule, it's better to be a plotter than a pantser when it comes to producing a tightly-crafted book. A plotter is someone who plots out their book in advance of writing, while a pantser tends to write on the fly. While flying by the seat of your pants may work for fiction writing, it's often better to have a plan in place for non-fiction writing.

Start by writing a short description of the book you intend to write, something that would go on the back cover to describe what a reader would get out of the book if they read it. Do a "brain dump" of everything you currently know about the subject and conduct any necessary research from outside sources. Identify the various stories, yours and others, for inclusion in the book. Pull together any existing content you have that could be incorporated into the book such as blog posts, articles, journals, videos, or audio transcripts. Flesh out the content for each chapter or section and write the first rough draft of the book.

After completing the first draft, put the book away for at least a week, then edit again, removing anything that doesn't support your book's core message. Wait another week, then do a second edit of your book. Seek feedback from friends, family, and trusted colleagues, noting the trends in the feedback such as "it was too slow" or "a particular section was confusing." Use this feedback to make any necessary changes and write the final rough draft of the book.

Finally, write and add an introduction, dedication and acknowledgement(s) to the book if desired. Make sure to determine if you need permission for any of the content you intend to include in the book before going to print, such as quotes from living people, copyrighted photos, and other images.

## Step 3: Packaging Your Book

Once your book is finished, it's important to review your working title and subtitle to ensure they still effectively convey the content and purpose of your book. You can also test different title and subtitle options on PickFu.com to see which one resonates better with your target audience.

Next, find, interview and hire a book cover designer or design agency to create an eye-catching and professional cover for your book. Decide on the trim size of your book and create a mock-up or provide examples of covers you like to your cover designer. Choose a publishing company name and purchase ISBNs for all versions of your book from Bowker (MyIdentifiers.com).

Hire a copy editor and proofreader to review your manuscript and make any necessary changes. Find someone to do interior design and formatting and get a well-recognized or connected person in your niche to write a foreword. Obtain book blurbs, quotes, and back cover copy for your book. Write three versions of your author bio, a short, medium, and long version.

Provide final page count to cover designer and get final cover for paperback and eBook. Identify the "hook" for your book, a 1-2 sentence summary that quickly explains what your book is about and why someone should read it. Proofread the entire book one last time and make final changes. Decide on the Amazon categories your book will be placed in and determine price points for all versions of your book. Identify and select seven marketing keywords.

Upload your book file to Amazon KDP (and/or other platforms), check the formatting of your eBook on at least two devices and order a physical proof to make sure the paperback looks good. Schedule a launch date and if you expect to sell or give away a large quantity of books, consider getting quotes from an offset printer to produce your book.

## Step 4: Launching Your Book

Alright, so now that your book is finished, it's time to start thinking about how to launch it. First, you'll want to put together a plan for your launch team. This includes figuring out who you want on the team, and how you'll find them. Your launch team should ideally be made up of around 10-20 people, who are part of your target reader audience. They'll provide feedback and write reviews in exchange for a free copy of your book before it's officially released.

Next, you may want to consider building a website for your book. This can be a great way to attract readers and make it easy for them to purchase your book. Your website should include an attention-grabbing header, a picture of your book with a link to Amazon, several positive reviews, a landing page and/or pop-up box for email capture, an "about the author" page, a "contact us" page, links to social media, and perhaps a "speaker" page with testimonials.

You'll also want to set up your Amazon Author Page and add your book to your author profile. To help determine who to market to, create a detailed "avatar" profile of your ideal reader, including things like age, gender, education, and profession. Create a spreadsheet of key influencers to approach for help, and contact them to see if there's a way you can help each other.

Provide copies of your book to your launch team, and aim to get 10-25 reviews within Amazon's rules. Decide if you want to use a .99 cent Kindle launch offer, and reach out to your personal network and existing platform to let them know the book is available for purchase.

You can also consider getting paid reviews from sources like Kirkus, BookBub, Author Buzz, and others. Keep track of your Amazon Best-Seller Rank daily, and call or email key contacts who agreed to help promote your book to give them updates and say thanks for their help. Finally, schedule social media posts on all your platforms with links and images to buy the book.

**Part 5: Promoting Your Book**

Prepare a digital media kit that includes a headshot of yourself, photos of the book, short and long author bio, book testimonials, speaking testimonials if you're seeking speaking engagements, and a list of possible interview questions.

- Launch your own podcast.
- Be a guest on other people's podcasts.
- Start and/or use an existing blog to share content from your book and promote it.

- Writing guest posts for other people's blogs.
- Create a Vlog (video blog on your site and post to YouTube).
- Create and publish an ongoing email newsletter (minimum once a month).
- Do a "blog tour."
- Reach out to book clubs.
- Contests/Give-a-ways (your own using Rafflecopter or via Amazon/Goodreads.)
- Social media posts (Twitter, Facebook, Instagram, Snapchat, LinkedIn) of content from or related to your book.
- Meme marketing – post images and text related to your book and topic using Pinterest, Facebook, and Instagram.
- Create a hashtag (#) around your book/topic.
- Set up a Facebook fan page and/or a Facebook Group.
- Do Facebook Lives sharing content or doing Q&A sessions. Repurpose to YouTube.
- Run Amazon ads (for more information, check out the book, *"Mastering Amazon Ads"* by Brian Meeks.
- Hire a publicity agency to secure media interviews (note: unless you have money to burn, be cautious—this can be effective, but it is also very expensive and does not guarantee results in terms of book sales).
- Write and send a press release.
- Hold an author event/book signing (at a book store or other event related to your topic.)
- Work at getting reviewed in mainstream publications and trade journals.
- Give free and/or paid speeches.
- Don't forget to optimize your website to feature your book and links to get it BEFORE the launch.
- Do a book marketing "swap" with other authors with similar reader affinity groups.
- Do author meet-ups.
- Networking opportunities.
- Partner with trade organizations / use a tradeshow booth.
- Leave thoughtful comments beneficial to others in the comment section on blogs with people discussing your general topic area.
- Ask local bookstores to offer your book for sale.

- Create a video series around the core concepts in your book with a link to buy it.
- Use paid book promotion services — (BookGorilla.com, ReadingDeals.com, BargainBooksy.com, Bookzio.com, JamesMayfield.com, BooksLoom.com, and others)
- Design and run Facebook ads or sponsor posts.
- Use a "Free Bonus with Book Purchase" strategy.
- Be a conference sponsor.
- Enter book contests (Axiom, Ben Franklin Awards, Christian Small Publisher Book of the Year Award, ForeWord Book Awards, IPPY Awards, National Indie Excellence Book Awards, Nautilus Book Awards, Next Generation Indie Book Awards, Writer's Digest Self- Published Book Awards, Indie Reader Discovery Awards, Reader Views Awards etc.)
- For more book promotion ideas, we recommend you read the following books: *Your First 1,000 Copies* by Tim Grahl; *Strangers to Superfans* by David Gaughran; *Market Like a Boss* by Honoree Corder (and, if you haven't read it yet, our book, *Million Dollar Book Formula*).

## Part 6: Post-Launch

A "Post-Launch Review" of the book writing, publishing, and marketing process should include the following:

- Reflecting on what could have been done better, such as additional editing or more effective marketing strategies.
- Identifying what went well, such as positive feedback from readers or strong sales.
- Recognizing unexpected challenges or opportunities that arose during the process.
- Continuing to promote the book to maintain momentum, such as through social media or book signings.
- Evaluating whether the book's success suggests the potential for a series.
- Sending written thank-you notes to everyone who helped with the book, both to express gratitude and to maintain relationships for future projects.

- Considering creating an audio version of the book, with the option to use resources such as the guide at milliondollarbookformula.com/audiobookreport.
- Planning for the next book, including researching potential topics and outlining a timeline for writing, publishing, and marketing.

 **FROM THE FIELD**

If you are wanting to write a book, but have never done it before, I highly suggest getting a "book coach".

**I recommend contacting Steve Gordon:**

https://writeyourmilliondollarbook.com/opt-in-page

"THERE ARE TWO KINDS OF PEOPLE, THOSE WHO DO THE WORK AND THOSE WHO TAKE THE CREDIT. TRY TO BE IN THE FIRST GROUP; THERE IS LESS COMPETITION THERE."

-INDIRA GANDHI

 # QR CODES

QR codes, or Quick Response codes, are two-dimensional barcodes that can be scanned using a smartphone camera or QR code reader app. They have become increasingly popular in recent years as a way for businesses to streamline their marketing and sales efforts.

One way that businesses can use QR codes for prospecting is by including them in their marketing materials, such as business cards, brochures, and even physical products. Here are a few ways that businesses can use QR codes for prospecting:

**Use QR codes to drive traffic to a landing page or website:**

By scanning the QR code, prospects can be directed to a specific page on your website or a landing page with more information about your product or service. This is a great way to capture leads and gather more information about your prospects.

**Offer special discounts or promotions:**

QR codes can be used to offer special discounts or promotions to prospects who scan the code. This can be a great way to entice prospects to make a purchase or sign up for a service.

**Provide easy access to product demonstrations or case studies:**

QR codes can be used to link to video demonstrations or case studies that show how your product or service can benefit prospects. This can be especially useful for complex products or services that may require more explanation.

**Share customer testimonials or reviews:**

QR codes can be used to link to customer testimonials or reviews, which can be a powerful way to build trust and credibility with prospects.

**Include QR codes on physical products:**

If you sell physical products, you can include QR codes on the packaging or on the product itself. This allows prospects to easily access more information about the product, such as instructions for use or care, or to leave a review or provide feedback.

Using QR codes for prospecting can be a simple and effective way to streamline your marketing and sales efforts. By including QR codes in your marketing materials and on physical products, you can provide prospects with easy access to more information and make it easier for them to take action.

But beware, using QR codes for prospecting can also have its pitfalls if not done correctly. Here are a few things to keep in mind when using QR codes:

**Make sure the QR code leads to a mobile-friendly page:**

Since most people will be scanning the QR code using their smartphones, it's important to make sure the page that the code leads to is mobile-friendly. If the page is difficult to navigate or takes too long to load, prospects may become frustrated and give up.

**Test the QR code before using it:**

Before including the QR code in your marketing materials, be sure to test it to make sure it works properly. There's nothing more frustrating for a prospect than scanning a QR code and being taken to a 404 error page.

**Use a good QR code reader app:**

If you're expecting prospects to scan your QR code, it's a good idea to recommend a good QR code reader app to use. This can help ensure that the code is scanned properly and the prospect is taken to the intended page.

**Incorporate QR codes into your overall marketing strategy:**

While QR codes can be a useful tool for prospecting, they should be just one piece of your overall marketing strategy. Don't rely solely on QR codes to reach prospects; be sure to use other tactics such as email marketing, social media, and content marketing as well.

By following these tips and using QR codes for prospecting in a smart and strategic way, you can effectively reach new prospects and drive more sales for your business. Happy scanning!

"I'VE NEVER BEEN POOR, ONLY BROKE.
BEING POOR IS A FRAME OF MIND.
BEING BROKE IS ONLY A
TEMPORARY SITUATION."

-MIKE TODD

# AUTOMATED SALES LEADS 24X7 USING AI

Wouldn't it be cool if you woke up in the morning, booted up your computer and found you had 100's of new sales leads waiting for you to follow up on? Sounds great, yes? AI Pixel Lead Tracking makes it possible.

Pixel tracking technology identifies who has visited your website, landing page, social media, and even YouTube! WebLeads.ai can identify visitors to your website, landing page, or social accounts without any action taken by the visitor – no form filled out, no number called- just visiting your page it will know who they are and populate a Google Sheets file with their info for you to follow up with. This technology works about 50-60% of the time.

**Here's what happens.**

Someone visits your website or landing page (or even social media); the pixel is alerted and then tracks down who that person is. It gathers their name, phone number, address, and email address. It then takes this information and does two things. One, it creates a Google Sheets file to organize the lead data, and two, automations can be set up so when the information is found the visitor is automatically sent an email with a lead magnet, or even a text message. Pretty cool, and to some a little scary. However, knowing who is visiting your website, you can proactively contact them and turn them into leads.

Website visitor tracking aims to gain insights into user behavior and preferences. This data can be used to improve user experience, understand customer needs, and target advertising. Examples of website tracking include understanding how users navigate a website, determining where users come from, remembering user preferences, and remembering the contents of a customer's shopping cart.

## How Does It Work?

Website visitor identification software typically uses different technologies to convert anonymous web traffic into leads. One of the primary ways is through deterministic matching. Deterministic matching uses a common identifier, such as a visitor's phone number or email address to match their activity across multiple devices back to a unique data record. This can help to identify anonymous visitors and collect contact information.

Pixel tracking, like that at WebLeads.ai, is a revolutionary piece of software that, once installed on your website, landing page, or sales funnel, will identify those who come from your social posts or paid advertisements and have an interest in your services. **This software is perfect for those who want to increase their lead generation and receive a large quantity of leads in a short amount of time**. In fact, many users have reported seeing a 3-6x increase in the number of leads they receive just 24 hours after installation.

But how does it work? An AI pixel is a small piece of code that is placed on a website and tracks visitors' behavior and activities. By analyzing the data collected by the pixel, an AI algorithm can identify patterns and trends that indicate a potential lead. For example, if a visitor spends a significant amount of time on a particular page, it may indicate that they are interested in that product or service. This information can then be used to reach out to the visitor and offer them more information or a sales pitch.

One of the great things about this technology is that it works wonderfully with a well-optimized CRM and automation system, or paired with a lead working call center, whether it's an internal or third-party call center. These leads are people who searched for your product, service or business, clicked on your advertisement or website, and interacted with your brand. These are high-intent leads that never submitted a form, but a highly effective strategy can be implemented to create a large success out of this cost-efficient program.

**Tracking Pixels vs. Cookies**

Pixel tracking and cookies are two methods used for website visitor tracking. Both methods involve collecting data about users' browsing habits, but they differ in how they collect and store data.

Cookies are small text files that are saved to a user's browser when they visit a website. They store information about a user's preferences and browsing history, which can be used to personalize the user's experience on the website. However, cookies can only be used to track a user on the device they are currently using, and users can choose to block or clear their cookies, rendering them useless.

On the other hand, tracking pixels are small images embedded in emails or web pages that can be used to track users across devices. When a user opens an email or visits a website that contains a tracking pixel, the pixel sends information back to the sender or website owner about the user's browsing habits.

Cookies can be blocked or deleted by the user, however, tracking pixels are harder to detect and remove.

**Different Kinds of Tracking Pixels**

- Retargeting Pixels
- Conversion Pixels
- Landing Page Pixel
- Facebook Pixel

**Common Website Tracking Methods**

There are several common website tracking methods, including cookies, pixels, tags, local storage, and web beacons. Each method has its own set of benefits and drawbacks, and each requires different levels of compliance with data privacy laws.

- **Cookies** are small text files that are stored on a user's device when they visit a website. They are used to remember a user's preferences, login information, and browsing history. They also allow for targeted advertising and remarketing. However, cookies also pose a privacy risk as they can be used to track a user's browsing activity across multiple websites. In the EU, cookies are regulated by the EU Cookie Directive, which requires website owners to obtain a user's consent before storing or accessing cookies on their device.

- **Pixels** are small images that are embedded on a website. They are used to track user behavior, such as which pages a user visit and how long they stay on a page. Pixels are often used in conjunction with cookies to track users across multiple websites. They also allow for targeted advertising and remarketing. Pixels can also be used to find visitor contact information – ***Prospecting on auto-pilot!***

- **Tags** are small pieces of code that are placed on a website to track user behavior. They are similar to pixels, but they are more flexible and can be used to track a wider range of user behavior. Tags can also be used to create custom tracking events, such as tracking clicks on a specific button or tracking when a user scrolls to a certain point on a page.

- **Local storage** is a method of storing data on a user's device. It is similar to cookies, but it allows for more data to be stored and for that data to be accessed even when a user is not on the website. Local storage can be used to remember a user's preferences, login information, and browsing history. However, it also poses a privacy risk as it can be used to track a user's browsing activity across multiple websites. Each of these tracking mechanisms has its own set of responsibilities and requirements when it comes to data privacy laws. For example, cookies are subject to specific regulations under the EU's cookie laws and must be clearly disclosed and consented to by users.

- **Web Beacons** are small transparent images that are embedded in a webpage or an email. They are used to track the user's behavior, such as which pages they visit or which links they click. Web beacons can also be used to track conversions, such as when a user makes a purchase or fills out a form.

## Compliance Challenges

The use of tracking pixels also raises compliance challenges, as they can potentially collect sensitive information, such as personal data and location, without the user's knowledge or consent. This can be a violation of data protection laws such as the General Data Protection Regulation (GDPR) and the California Consumer Privacy Act (CCPA).

As such, it is important for website owners, marketers, and advertisers to be aware of the laws and regulations surrounding the use of tracking pixels and to implement proper consent mechanisms and data protection measures to ensure compliance.

Website owners and marketers should be transparent about the use of tracking pixels and provide clear, concise information about their use and data collection practices in their privacy policy. They should also implement proper consent mechanisms and data protection measures to ensure compliance with data protection laws such as the GDPR and CCPA.

## How Can You Legally Track Website Visitors?

**Pixel tracking is not illegal**. However, website tracking must comply with data privacy laws, which generally take one of two approaches: opt-in or opt-out. Opt-in requires explicit consent from users before tracking them, while opt-out allows tracking unless the user requests to stop. Opt-in requires consent before tracking, while opt-out allows tracking until the user requests to stop. **I'm not a lawyer, but in my experience, if you have a strong privacy policy and/or a site terms pop up that must be clicked you are ok.**

 FROM THE FIELD

Pixel tracking can be a valuable tool for businesses looking to improve their sales pipeline and marketing efforts. In most cases *new sales*

*leads can be grown 5x-10x on auto-pilot,* in a very short amount of time, compared to other prospecting methods.

## Automated Sales Lead Prospecting 24x7 – WebLeads.ai

What's cool about WebLeads.ai is they take AI Pixel Tracking to a whole new level. Once they identify a prospect via their AI Pixel, they can set up different automations to promote your nurturing sequence or lead magnet to that prospect.

Prospect information that is automatically sent to your preferred CRM or Google Sheets include:

- First Name
- Last Name
- Email Address
- Mobile Phone
- Postal Address
- URL They Visited On Your Website

For instance, traffic hits your website, landing page, or social pages (coming from paid ads, your social media accounts, a guest blog post you did, etc.). WebLeads.ai identifies a prospect (without them doing anything, no form fill out, no call, just landing on your page), it could then send them an introductory email, then maybe wait a few days and send another, then perhaps wait a week and send a SMS message with a link to your calendar, or even a link to your YouTube channel. All automated 24x7. They build automated sales prospecting machines that 5x–10x your prospect list, and they do it custom to your target audience.

Very cool.

Go check out www.WebLeads.ai to see how all of this works.

 # GO MAKE MONEY!

The power of being good at prospecting cannot be underestimated. A good client prospector is not only able to sell products or services effectively, but they also can build long-lasting relationships with their customers and earn their trust. In today's competitive market, it's crucial for businesses to have client prospectors who are skilled and capable of adapting to the needs and preferences of their clients.

**Here are some key qualities and techniques that every good client prospector should possess:**

### Commitment:

A good client prospector is fully committed to their job and always puts their best effort into every sale. They understand the importance of building relationships with their clients and are willing to go the extra mile to ensure their satisfaction.

### Honesty and straightforwardness:

Good client prospectors are honest and straightforward in their dealings with clients. They don't try to manipulate or deceive their customers in any way, but rather provide them with accurate and reliable information about the products or services they are selling.

### Good listening skills:

A good client prospector is a good listener. They listen attentively to their clients' needs and concerns, and are able to understand their unique perspectives and requirements. This allows them to tailor their sales pitch to the specific needs of each individual client.

## Self-confidence:

Self-confidence is a crucial quality for any good client prospector. It enables them to believe in their own abilities and the products or services they are selling, and to communicate that belief to their clients.

## Persistence:

Good client prospectors are persistent and don't give up easily. They understand that not every sale will be successful, but they don't let setbacks discourage them. Instead, they keep trying and use each experience as an opportunity to learn and improve.

The power of good client prospector qualities and techniques lies in their ability to build strong relationships with their clients, communicate effectively, and persist in the face of challenges. By developing these skills, client prospectors can be instrumental in helping businesses grow and succeed.

## Here is a quick step-by-step breakdown of what this book has outlined:

1. **Define your ideal customer:** Start by creating a detailed customer profile that includes demographics, pain points, and buying habits. This will help you identify potential prospects who are most likely to be interested in your products or services.
2. **Research potential prospects:** Use various online tools and resources to find and gather information about potential prospects. This can include social media, professional networking sites, and industry databases.
3. **Create a list of potential prospects:** Organize the information you've gathered and create a list of potential prospects that match your customer profile.
4. **Reach out to potential prospects:** Use a variety of methods to initiate contact with potential prospects, such as cold emailing, ask them to be a guest on your podcast or YouTube channel, and social media outreach.

5. **Qualify potential prospects:** During initial contact, ask questions and gather information to determine if the potential prospect is a good fit for your products or services.
6. **Build relationships:** Continue to engage with potential prospects through regular communication, such as follow-up calls or emails, to build relationships and establish trust.
7. **Identify decision-makers:** As you continue to build relationships, take note of any decision-makers within the organization and make sure to include them in your communication efforts.
8. **Present your solution:** Once you have established a relationship and identified decision-makers, present your solution and explain how it can benefit the potential prospect.
9. **Close the deal:** Use the information and relationships you've built to close the deal and secure new business.
10. **Continuously prospect:** Remember that prospecting is an ongoing process and continue to search for new potential prospects to ensure a steady pipeline of new business.

I hope you have found this guide as an inspirational resource for your prospecting efforts. No book can walk you step by step through every single tip or process, but I hope you use the ideas in this book to do further research on some of the different techniques I outlined. Some of these ideas won't work for your business, others will lead you down the road to having the most successful year you have ever had! Also, please remember, I barely touched on **ALL** of the different ways to prospect for new clients, the ones in this book are just the ones that have worked for me.

I wish you the best of luck on honing your prospecting skills, and don't forget to visit www.ProspectingHacks.com to get your free guides!

**Good luck using this guide! Go make money!**

*illegitimis non carborundum*

"AFTER YOU ASK A CLOSING QUESTION, SHUT UP! THE NEXT PERSON WHO SPEAKS LOSES."

-JEFFREY GITOMER

Made in the USA
Middletown, DE
24 April 2023

29425277R00129